D1575781

"But aren't you even afraid, Mr. Houdini?" one of the reporters shouted to him.

"Afraid?" Houdini asked with a loud laugh. "What do I have to fear? I am the King of Handcuffs. Nothing can hold me!"

"But the freezing temperatures, sir. The iron chains . . . how . . . ?"

But Houdini just grinned and kept walking. The policeman next to Houdini leaned close to him and said in a low voice, "Don't be a fool. This is suicide! There's still time to change your mind."

"Never," Houdini replied with the slightest of a frown and continued toward the river.

A Background Note about
THE AMAZING HARRY HOUDINI

More than eighty years after the death of Harry Houdini, we still say that a person has "pulled a Houdini" when that person escapes from what seems like an impossible situation. Harry Houdini was known as "The Handcuff King," but his escapes went far beyond handcuffs. Prison cells, locked coffins, sealed water tanks, and even the belly of a sea monster could not hold Houdini. His amazing abilities made him one of the most famous men on earth in the early 1900s.

But Harry Houdini's rise to fame was not an easy one. Born into a poor family, Houdini was one of five children. Before he was even ten years old, Houdini was working long, hard days at boring jobs. But as he shined shoes and delivered papers, he began dreaming of becoming a magician. And that dream never died. Houdini struggled for years doing his shows at back-alley bars and low-paying circuses. Still, Harry Houdini knew that one day the entire world would know his name. And one day, it did.

The Amazing Harry Houdini traces Houdini's amazing journey from rags to riches and beyond. Not satisfied being just a magician and escape artist, Houdini was also a pilot, an author, a movie star, and the original "ghostbuster." Today, thousands of people still remain loyal Houdini followers with museums and fan clubs worldwide. And many fans of the magician still gather every year on the anniversary of his death. Holding séances and looking for a sign from their hero, they hope for one last bit of magic from The Great Houdini.

The Amazing
HARRY HOUDINI

TANYA SAVORY

TP THE TOWNSEND LIBRARY

THE AMAZING
HARRY HOUDINI

TP **THE TOWNSEND LIBRARY**

For more titles in the Townsend Library,
visit our website: **www.townsendpress.com**

All new material in this edition is
copyright © 2009 by Townsend Press.
Printed in the United States of America

0 9 8 7 6 5 4 3 2 1

Illustrations copyright © 2009 by Hal Taylor

Townsend Press, Inc.
439 Kelley Drive
West Berlin, NJ 08091
cs@townsendpress.com

ISBN-13: 978-1-59194-175-0
ISBN-10: 1-59194-175-X

Library of Congress Control Number:
2008932212

CONTENTS

CHAPTER 1

On a cold spring morning in Boston in 1908, thousands of people waited patiently outside a fancy hotel. The crowd was mostly quiet, except for occasional murmurings: "How will he do it?" "Surely he'll die this time." "He must be crazy." Four policemen, frowning and looking at their watches, stood on the front steps of the hotel. One of the officers held two pairs of handcuffs, and another had two heavy chains slung over his shoulder. As the minutes ticked by, the officers just looked at one another and shook their heads.

Suddenly, the front door of the hotel flew open. A short man with curly hair and a wide smile waved with both arms to the crowd. "I am The Great Houdini!" he shouted dramatically as the crowd burst into cheers and whistles. Flashbulbs popped, and newspaper reporters pushed and shoved their way through the crowd in an effort to get to this little man who called himself "Houdini." But the police were already surrounding him in a tight circle. They gripped Houdini's shoulders and led him quickly through the admiring crowd. Men tried to slap Houdini on the back and shake his hand. Children stared in awe and tried to touch his long black coat as he moved past them. A few women fainted.

Down the street and toward the Charles River, the whole procession moved like a strange parade. Those who had not been able to join the party watched from windows or shivered on rooftops with spyglasses. Somewhere near the river, a band was playing lively music. When Houdini heard the music, he smiled even more broadly and tapped his gold-tipped cane in time with the songs.

"But aren't you even afraid, Mr. Houdini?" one of the reporters shouted to him.

"Afraid?" Houdini asked with a loud laugh. "What do I have to fear? I am the King of Handcuffs. Nothing can hold me!"

"But the freezing temperatures, sir. The iron chains . . . how . . . ?"

Houdini just grinned and kept walking. The policeman next to Houdini leaned close to him and said in a low voice, "Don't be a fool. This is suicide! There's still time to change your mind."

"Never," Houdini replied with the slightest frown and continued toward the river.

Eventually, Houdini and the crowd, which had now grown to nearly 10,000 people, reached the stone bridge that crossed the Charles River. Below the bridge, many more people had gathered in rowboats, canoes, and even rafts. The police escorted Houdini to the top of the bridge near the railing and cleared a small space around him. Hopping on top of a wooden crate, Houdini raised his hands. Immediately, the crowd was silent.

"Ladies and gentlemen! I have examined the handcuffs that Sergeant Fields is about to place on me. I can assure you that these are strong regulation handcuffs made to restrain criminals and dangerous men. If there is any one of you today that does not believe that these are real handcuffs, please feel free to come forward and examine them for yourself."

Houdini waited calmly for any doubting member of the crowd to come forward, but no one did. The sergeant raised the heavy cuffs high into the air for all to see. Another officer raised the chains and shook them a bit for effect.

"All right, then," Houdini finally shouted. "Let us proceed."

With that, Houdini whipped off his hat with a flourish and sent it sailing out over the water. Next, he slipped out of his long black coat. Then he leaned down to untie his shoes. Off came both shoes and then his socks. Next, his tie and crisp white shirt were tossed into the growing pile of clothes next to him. When Houdini reached for his belt buckle, laughter erupted from some in the crowd, as whistles and cheers egged Houdini on. Mothers covered their children's eyes. Finally, Houdini stood before the thousands of spectators, wearing nothing but a tiny pair of swimming trunks.

"Gentlemen, if you will," Houdini said, bowing to the policemen. This was his invitation to be searched. For several minutes the officers searched every inch of Houdini for anything he might use to unlock the handcuffs—a small key or even a tiny piece of wire. They pulled and prodded his hair, looked in his mouth and poked at his teeth with a small metal stick, and even checked the soles of his feet and between his toes. In the end, the police shrugged their shoulders, scratched their heads, and admitted that they could find nothing.

And then Houdini was shackled.

As the crowd watched in nervous silence, Sergeant Fields pulled Houdini's arms tightly behind his back and snapped together the two sets of handcuffs—one on his wrists and another on his forearms. Then another officer stepped forward to attach heavy chains from Houdini's wrists to thick irons on his ankles. In all, the weight of the chains and cuffs was nearly thirty pounds.

"And now, ladies and gentlemen," Houdini cried out with great emotion, "the moment has come! It is the time for me to risk everything. But first . . ."

Houdini looked into the crowd and locked eyes with a pretty woman who smiled back at him. But there were also tears of worry in her eyes. It was Houdini's wife, Bess. Quickly, she came forward and put her arms around her husband, giving him a kiss for good luck. The crowd cheered and whistled as the kiss lingered. Then Houdini nodded confidently toward the crowd and turned toward the river. For only a moment, he looked down at the cold, dark water rushing by sixty feet below. Then, as 10,000 onlookers gasped in fear, Houdini jumped off the bridge.

Down, down through freezing darkness, the weight of the chains and cuffs dragged Houdini to the bottom of the river in seconds. As he landed with a soundless thud on the rocks of the river's floor, all Houdini could hear was his own heart beating. Far above him, he could barely make out the dim greenish light of the water's surface. The river's current was stronger than he had expected—it was already beginning to pull him away. *One hundred and seventy-five seconds*, Houdini thought to himself. This was as long as he could hold his breath. There was no time to waste.

Along the riverbanks and on the bridge, the crowd seemed to be holding its breath too. The band played a cheery tune, but as the seconds ticked by, the faces of the spectators grew more and more worried. After one minute, a man in the crowd yelled, "For God's sake, someone help him! He's drowning!" Thirty seconds later, a policeman shouted, "Something's gone wrong—go after him!" to one of Houdini's assistants who waited in a small boat beneath the bridge. But the assistant just smiled calmly and shook his head.

But when two minutes and fifteen seconds had passed, even the assistant began to look pale. Houdini's wife sat on the wooden crate with her head in her hands. And the shouts and screams from the crowd were louder than the band as men shook their fists and children burst into tears.

Suddenly, the sun came out from behind the clouds and shone brilliantly, like a spotlight, on the water. And at that very moment, Houdini exploded through the surface with a huge exhalation of air. For a second, the crowd was so stunned and relieved that they couldn't make a sound. Then, grinning widely, Houdini raised two sets of opened handcuffs over his head, and the crowd went wild. Thunderous cheering and clapping filled the air. Total strangers hugged each other, and several more women fainted. Houdini had done it again—he had escaped certain death.

How *had* Houdini done it? No one has ever known for certain. However, in his day, and even one hundred years later, there were and are many theories. Some people believed that Houdini understood locks and handcuffs so well that he knew exactly how to tap them against a hard surface (like the rocks at the bottom of a river) to open them. Others believed that Bess's kiss was not just for good luck. In her mouth, perhaps, was a small key that she passed to Houdini during their long kiss "goodbye." Still others believed something else entirely. They believed that Houdini knew something that no one else knew, that he had been given a most unusual gift—the gift of magic.

The evening following Houdini's handcuffed jump from the Charles River Bridge, his show at the largest theater in Boston was completely sold out. Over the course of many years, Houdini had become a superstar. Everyone, even worldwide, wanted to see the man who could escape from chains, walk through walls, swallow needles, and even make an elephant disappear.

Houdini, dressed in a fine silk suit and wearing gold cufflinks, walked onstage to deafening

applause and took a deep bow. As he straight-
ened up, his gaze traveled across the cheering
audience until his eyes fell upon a young boy.
The boy was dressed poorly and was sitting next
to his father in the cheapest seats. But on the
boy's face was an expression of utter awe and
wonderment. Before the lights dimmed and
the show began, Houdini's and the boy's eyes
met for a brief moment. And in that moment,
Houdini was taken back to a different time—a
time long before silk suits, packed theaters, and
fame and fortune.

CHAPTER 2

"**E**hrich! Get down from there! You'll kill yourself if you fall," Mrs. Weiss shouted out the window to her seven-year-old son. Ehrich pretended that he hadn't heard his mother and continued trying to tie a rope between two trees about fifteen feet up in the air. The problem was not climbing the trees and tying the rope—the problem was getting the rope tight enough. It couldn't sag at all, or else it would be a disaster.

"Ehrich!" Mrs. Weiss had walked into the backyard and was standing directly beneath the tree.

"But Ma," Ehrich sighed. "I have to practice. I won't get hurt."

"I don't know what you're planning on 'practicing,' but you're not doing it up there," his mother responded, her arms folded across her chest.

Ehrich knew better than to disobey his mother, but this time it was just too important.

"But it'll only take me a little while to get good. And then," Ehrich added quietly, looking down at his mother carefully, "I will earn lots of money for us."

Mrs. Weiss looked up and shook her head. It had not been an easy couple of years for the Weiss family. Mr. Weiss had found a job as a rabbi, but it did not bring in nearly enough money for a family of eight, with five sons and one daughter. The Weisses had moved to the United States from Hungary only a few years earlier, in 1876, when hatred toward Jewish people like the Weisses had become so strong that Ehrich's parents feared for their children's futures. Things were safer and more welcoming in the United States, but it was very hard for a man who spoke little English to earn a decent living. And quite often there was not enough to eat.

As Ehrich's mother stood below, momentarily lost in thought, Ehrich worked quickly to tighten the ropes. *I know I can do this*, he thought fiercely. The night before, Ehrich had gone to a circus with his father. Although the Weisses barely had any money to spare, the cheapest seats (in the back near the animal cages) were only a nickel. Ehrich had saved ten cents from his paper delivery job and had asked his father to go with him.

Throughout the circus show, Ehrich was

slightly entertained by the clowns and the animals and the loud music. But near the end of the show, Ehrich saw something that astounded him. High above the audience, a small man dressed in tights stood on a platform next to a rope that stretched half the length of the circus tent. Suddenly, the man began to walk across the rope, balancing himself with a pole. Falling would certainly mean broken bones . . . or worse. The crowd was absolutely quiet as they watched. *This is what everyone was waiting for*, Ehrich thought. *This is why they bought tickets—they want to see him risk his life!* It was something that young Ehrich Weiss would never forget.

And so now, before his mother could stop him, Ehrich stepped out onto his homemade tightrope. His mother held her breath as she watched her son slowly inch along the rope, using a broomstick for balance. Just when it looked as though Ehrich would make it to the other side, he glanced down to make sure his mother was watching. Suddenly, Ehrich teetered, panicked, and came tumbling down. But except for knocking out a baby tooth that had been loose anyway, he was unhurt. "I did it!" he shouted. "I am Ehrich the Great!"

And although his mother protested, Ehrich had soon mastered tightrope walking. True to his words to his mother, Ehrich began charging the neighborhood children a penny apiece to witness his amazing and death-defying act. And after every show, he proudly handed his mother every penny. At the tender age of seven, Ehrich had entered the world of show business.

But within a few years, even harder times hit the Weiss family. Ehrich's father was a good rabbi, but his English had never improved very much. At first, the congregation had been charmed by this highly educated rabbi from the Old World. They assumed that his English would get better as time went by, and they waited patiently. But now the congregation had grown restless. Slowly, they began discussing finding a rabbi who could speak better. Then one day, Mr. Weiss was fired. Try as he might, he could not find another job. He was a well-educated and very intelligent man, but no one seemed interested in hiring a Hungarian rabbi who spoke little English. Ehrich and his four brothers would have to find real jobs—the days of backyard circus acts were over.

Only ten years old, Ehrich worked long hours shining shoes in front of a fancy hotel and selling newspapers when there were no shoeshine customers. Wisconsin, where the Weisses lived, had bitterly cold winters, but Ehrich headed over to the hotel every day after school and rarely complained. He and his brothers combined all their earnings at the end of every day, counting all the pennies and nickels and handing them to their oldest brother, Theo, to give to their mother. On a very good day, usually a Saturday, they might earn two dollars altogether.

On one of their very good Saturdays, Theo counted up the money as usual and tucked it in his coat pocket. At that moment, a friend came by with a sled and offered Theo and Ehrich a quick ride home along the icy roads. Both boys gladly accepted. But when they got home, Theo reached for the money in his pocket and, to his great dismay, realized that it had all fallen out on the way home. Mrs. Weiss burst into tears. More than anything, Ehrich hated to see his mother sad. He rushed to her side, tears in his own eyes, and promised her that he and Theo would find the money.

However, an hour of searching along the dark and icy road turned up only one nickel. The two brothers slumped down on the side of the road in a snow pile, trying to figure out what to do. It was dinnertime, and the Saturday night streets were packed with couples on their way to restaurants or parties.

"I have an idea," Ehrich finally said. "Hand me that nickel. I can turn it into two dollars."

"You're crazy," Theo replied irritably. "You're not a magician."

"Just watch," Ehrich said as he grabbed the nickel and ran across the road to a flower shop. Ehrich bought a flower for a nickel and ran up to the first young man he saw walking along with a young woman. In seconds, Ehrich had sold the flower for a dime. Dashing back to the flower shop, he bought two more flowers and handed one to Theo, explaining what to do. In no time at all, the brothers had made back all the lost money.

"Well," said Theo on the walk back home, "that wasn't magic, but it was pretty close."

The following spring, Ehrich began working as an apprentice for a locksmith named Mr. Hanauer. It wasn't exactly exciting work for a young boy, but it paid more than shining shoes. However, one afternoon something happened that was exciting—something that would stay with Ehrich the rest of his life. At just about lunchtime, the town sheriff walked into the shop with a prisoner who had served his time and was being released. But around the prisoner's wrists was a pair of heavy handcuffs.

"Key broke off in the lock," the sheriff explained. "Looks like you'll have to saw them off."

"Here, Ehrich," Mr. Hanauer said, handing him a hacksaw. "You do it. I'm going to lunch." And with that, the sheriff and Ehrich's boss walked out the door, leaving eleven-year-old Ehrich with a tiny hacksaw and an angry and impatient 250-pound man.

"You had better be extra careful with that saw, sonny," the man said threateningly. "You cut me, and we're gonna have a problem."

Six times, Ehrich tried to saw through the cuffs, and six times the blade broke in two and had to be replaced. Finally, hands shaking, Ehrich decided to take a different approach. Ehrich knew that sometimes a hook or wire could be used to pick handcuffs. If he could find an extremely thin wire that would fit around the broken key, and if he moved the wire very carefully in just the right way, maybe . . . just maybe . . .

Click! The handcuffs popped open on Ehrich's first try. At that very moment, Mr. Hanauer and the sheriff walked in. There stood Ehrich with the jammed cuffs—removed from the prisoner but still in one piece.

"That's amazing!" Mr. Hanauer exclaimed, looking back and forth from the cuffs to the thin wire still in Ehrich's other hand. "Looks like you've got quite a future in locks."

Ehrich just smiled and nodded. Little did he know just how true his boss's words would be.

From that point on, Ehrich became fascinated with opening locks, planning escapes, and figuring out how magicians did their tricks. When he wasn't working, Ehrich spent hours—sometimes all night long—reading books about magicians. He began to understand that the "magic" tricks performed were only illusions—something that appeared to be real but wasn't. Ehrich was occasionally allowed to spend a nickel to attend the traveling magic shows that passed through town. He sat in the cheap seats, totally absorbed in every little movement of the magician. *I know how he does that!* Ehrich would think to himself. But one night, he wasn't so sure.

"Tonight, ladies and gentlemen, I am going to cut my assistant into pieces," the tall magician named Dr. Lynn bellowed to the crowd. With this, he placed a thin, nervous-looking man into a box with his head, arms, and legs sticking out. The assistant waved to the crowd and kicked his legs in order to prove that these were, in fact, his real limbs. Then a black bag was placed over the assistant's head.

Dr. Lynn dramatically swung a sword through the air as he approached the man in the box.

"What first?" he shouted. And without waiting for an answer, he lopped off both of the man's arms and handed them to other assistants. As quickly, he chopped off the legs and then the head, which went bouncing across the stage in its black bag. The audience, including Ehrich, gasped in horror. It looked so real!

But before the head rolled off the stage, Dr. Lynn picked it up and carried it back to its owner. Placing it back exactly where the assistant's head had been, he removed the black bag and, magically, there was the assistant smiling and blinking at the audience. Next, Dr. Lynn collected the arms and legs and shoved them back into the box with the assistant. "Put yourself together," he barked. In seconds, the assistant was whole again and waving to the stunned audience.

For days, Ehrich could think of nothing but this "magic." And he vowed that he would not stop thinking about it, or searching for books that explained it, until he figured it out.

About the time Ehrich became a teenager, his life changed completely. His father, who had never been able to find another real job in Wisconsin, decided that moving the family to New York City would provide many more job opportunities and a better place to live. He was wrong. Not only were jobs harder to find, but now the rent was higher and the food more expensive. More than a few times, the family had to move from one apartment to another when they could not pay the rent. Once again, Ehrich was faced with finding a job to help pay the bills. The only job he could get was that of a messenger boy—a job that barely paid more than a handful of tips a day.

However, as always, Ehrich used his quick thinking and charm to pull in a little more cash. As Christmas grew near and the crowds along the busy city streets were more and more filled with holiday spirit, Ehrich pinned a sign to his hat that read:

Christmas is coming,
Turkeys are fat,
Please drop a quarter
in the messenger boy's hat.

A messenger boy's hat was a large hat full of creases and edges, so Ehrich kept his hat (and sign) on his head, hoping that people would tuck quarters in the creases as he worked. His regular customers laughed out loud at the sign and were glad to give a little extra Christmas tip. And even strangers on the street dug in their pockets for change. By day's end, Ehrich had dozens of quarters. He hid them in his hair, up his sleeves, and behind his ears. When he got home, he walked over to his mother and said, "Shake me. I'm magic." Mrs. Weiss laughed and gave her son a strange look. But when she gave him a shake, all those quarters suddenly came tumbling out. When they were counted, it was just enough to finish paying the rent. The Weiss family would not have to move before Christmas after all.

As Ehrich grew older, along with his obsession with magic, he also became obsessed with sports. Although he was short, only 5 feet, 4 inches, he was unusually strong and ultra-competitive. Ehrich could not bear being beaten at anything— not by a magician's trick and not by another runner in a race through Central Park. By his mid-teens, Ehrich won every race he entered, from sprints to long distance. In his mind, to be second best at anything was unacceptable.

In keeping with his determination to succeed, Ehrich woke up one morning and decided that he needed a better job. As he wandered through the busy city streets looking for "help wanted" signs, he saw a long line of young men standing behind a sign that read: "Assistant Necktie Cutter Wanted." With an official air, Ehrich walked over, picked up the sign, and tucked it under his arm.

"Thank you for coming," Ehrich said in an official tone, "but I regret to inform you that this position has been filled." With that, the men walked away, grumbling. Immediately, Ehrich went inside, informed the employer that he was the only applicant, and was hired right away.

But, of course, cutting neckties was not Ehrich's dream. More and more, he was being drawn into the fascinating world of magic and how it was performed. Luckily for Ehrich, one of his coworkers, a young man named Jacob Hyman, was also very interested in magic. Together, they would practice card tricks and coin tricks at work until the performances were flawless. Even at the family dinner table at night, Ehrich would have a fork in one hand and cards in the other.

It was Jacob who encouraged his friend to start performing at little venues around New York City. And it was Jacob who lent Ehrich a book that changed his life. The book, *Memoirs of Robert-Houdin*, was the story of one of the most talented and famous magicians who had ever lived: Jean Eugene Robert-Houdin. Houdin, a Frenchman, had been the first magician to present magic as an art form, not just as a cheap stunt in a traveling circus. Houdin made things disappear and reappear. He conjured up wine bottles that were never empty, no matter how many glasses they poured. He presented orange trees that grew from a seed to a tree in mere minutes. He charmed audiences, and even kings and queens, worldwide.

Ehrich stayed up the entire night reading about Houdin. In the morning, he handed the book back to Jacob.

"I want nothing more of my life than to become like Houdin," Ehrich said solemnly.

Jacob knew his friend was serious. "Well," Jacob said thoughtfully, "in the French language, adding the letter 'i' to a name means 'like' that person. You should call yourself 'Houdini.' It would mean 'like Houdin.'"

Ehrich thought this was a brilliant idea. But he would also need a new first name. Around his house, his nickname had always been "Harry." This would fit well with "Houdini." So on that morning in 1891, a simple yet somewhat magical transformation took place—Ehrich Weiss became Harry Houdini.

CHAPTER 3

Harry and Jacob worked quickly cutting out neckties from the material in front of them. Harry glanced around the room to make sure their boss wasn't nearby. Lately, the boss had noticed that the two boys had cards and coins in their hands as often as necktie material, and he wasn't too happy about it. Seeing that the coast was clear, Harry leaned toward Jacob.

"Come on! I *know* we can do it. We're good," Harry whispered.

Jacob kept working. His only response was to slightly shake his head.

"But why not?" Harry asked. "You don't want to be a necktie cutter for the rest of your life, do you?"

Jacob sighed and looked at his friend. "Harry, we can't make a living doing magic shows."

"But how will we know until we've tried?"

Harry insisted. "Plus," Harry added confidently, "I have no doubt we'll be famous. And rich. 'The Brothers Houdini'—everyone will know our name before long."

For several months, Harry and Jacob had been playing shows around the city. The shows were short and simple: a few card and coin tricks, flowers that suddenly appeared in their hands, and silk scarves that seemed to be pulled from their ears. Billing themselves as "The Brothers Houdini," the two friends were not exactly in big demand, and the "shows" they did were mostly birthday parties or street-corner performances. But Harry had caught the show-business bug. Now he wanted to quit the tie-cutting job to pursue magic fulltime. And he wanted Jacob to quit too.

"But what if we fail?" Jacob whispered. "What if no one wants to book us?"

Harry frowned. Giving up before even trying was something he was unfamiliar with. "We *won't* fail! Everyone loves our show—we'll have so many bookings that we'll have to turn half of them down!"

The friends whispered back and forth for most of the afternoon. Jacob was not at all sure that quitting a secure job would be a wise idea. But when five o'clock rolled around, Harry turned in his notice. And so did Jacob. The Brothers Houdini were in business.

But right from the start, business was hard. Harry did his best to talk theater owners into booking the act, but the owners laughed in his face. "Go to the dives, kid," they barked. "No one knows who you are. Theaters are for the professionals." So Harry set his sights a bit lower, swallowed his pride, and looked into performing at the "dives." These were the back-alley bars where late-night entertainment was needed to keep the people in the bars and ordering drinks. These were also the "dime museums." Dime museums were small buildings that presented what were known as the "freaks" and the "geeks." But those words had different meanings back in the late 1800s. "Freaks" referred to people (and sometimes animals) that were unusual or deformed: a bearded lady, a man with seven fingers, a goat with five legs, very short and very tall people, and even twins joined together. "Geeks," on the other hand, referred to people who could do something unusual like singing, dancing, or magic. Houdini was a geek.

Jacob didn't last very long. He didn't particularly like the atmosphere of the dime museums. They were considered by many to be low-class and not a place that anyone with money, education, or manners would visit. But the bars were even worse. As the crowds got drunk and rowdy, they would begin throwing pennies and even beer at the entertainers. It was not uncommon for a drunk patron to teeter over to Houdini or Jacob and start pulling their hair and prodding at them to try and figure out where cards or coins were hidden. After only a few weeks of show business, Jacob announced that he was returning to tie-cutting. Houdini was on his own.

Houdini was on his eighth show of the day at the dime museum on West 42nd Street. Since new customers passed through all day long, Houdini often did up to twenty shows a day. Suddenly, a messenger ran up to Houdini.

"Hey, are you that Houdini magician?"

Harry nodded.

"Well, you'd better go home. Your father's dying."

Without a word, Harry threw his cards and coins into a sack and sprinted toward home. His father had been ill with cancer for weeks. The family had prayed that he would recover, but he had only continued to worsen day by day. Now the end was near. With tears streaming down his face, Harry bounded up the stairs to the family's tiny apartment and rushed to his father's side. He grabbed his father's hand, and Mr. Weiss slowly opened his bloodshot eyes. The rest of the family stood around the bed solemnly.

"Ehrich? Ehrich, is it you?" his father whispered hoarsely.

"Yes, Papa. I'm here."

His father breathed raggedly as though trying to summon the energy to say a few words.

"You must promise me," he finally whispered,
"promise to take care of your mother. Never let
her want for anything." Although Ehrich was not
the oldest son, he was the one that Mr. Weiss felt
was most responsible and capable of taking care
of Mrs. Weiss in her older years.

"Of course, Papa. Of course I promise."

Mr. Weiss gripped his son's hand with the
little energy he had left. Then, in a voice that
could barely be heard, he said his last words:
"Don't ever forget your promise."

If Harry Houdini had been determined to
succeed before, he was now twice as determined.
Doing card tricks in the dime museums had
sharpened some of his skills and gotten him used
to performing, but he knew that his act must be
more exciting and more unique if he was going
to be a success. Harry's brother, Theo, had
begun to share the same fascination with magic,
so not long after their father's death, Harry
approached Theo.

"How much money do you have saved?"
Harry asked casually.

Theo gave his brother a strange look. "About
fourteen dollars. Why?"

"I'm wondering . . ." Harry began and then
paused dramatically, clasping his hands together

and staring hard at his brother. "I'm wondering if you would like to invest that money in our future together as the real 'Brothers Houdini.'"

Theo thought about this for several moments. Fourteen dollars was a pretty good chunk of money in 1893. It was roughly equal to $150 in today's money. But Theo greatly admired his brother's talents. Being asked to go into performing together was an honor. Still, fourteen dollars . . .

"What do we need that kind of money for?" Theo finally asked.

Harry smiled. That question was as good as a "yes" from Theo. He walked over and put his hand on Theo's shoulder. "Come with me and see."

The brothers walked several blocks and then down a strange, dark alley until they came to the door of a retired magician. The old man ushered them into a candlelit backroom that was full of magician's tools, props, and a stack of dusty books. Harry pointed to a battered old trunk in the corner.

"Ah, yes," the old man said, with a sad smile and a theatrical wave of his hand. "That was my greatest trick. Quite mysterious. Quite baffling indeed." Then the man cleared his throat and, in an entirely different tone of voice, announced, "Ten dollars. Cash."

Harry handed the old magician ten dollars of Theo's money.

"Two dollars for the stack of books?" Harry asked politely.

"Six," the magician said flatly.

"How about four?"

The old man grumbled but agreed. And Harry and Theo grabbed their treasures and dashed out—happy and flat broke.

"Ladies and gentlemen, what you are about to witness will astound you," Houdini said to the large crowd that had gathered at the dime museum. "The transformation that is about to happen is truly magical. I call it—" and here Houdini paused for emphasis—"The Metamorphosis!"

And here's what happened: First, Houdini invited anyone and everyone in the audience to come up and examine the old trunk he and Theo had bought from the magician. They were welcome to look inside it, touch it, and check as closely as they wanted for any hidden keys or tools. Next, Theo handcuffed Houdini's hands tightly behind his back. Houdini was then stuffed inside a big burlap bag that was double-tied at the top. Then the bag containing Houdini was placed inside the trunk.

At this point, Theo closed the lid of the trunk. He then invited several audience members to come up and place six locks around the lid, close them, and make sure they were locked. Theo then pulled a curtain in front of the trunk and stepped behind it shouting, "Behold! A miracle!" He clapped his hands three times; and only a few seconds after the third clap, out stepped Houdini around the curtain—untied, out of the bag, and out of the locked trunk.

But where was Theo? Pushing the curtain aside, Houdini unlocked all six locks on the trunk with a master key handed to him by an assistant. Then he lifted up the burlap bag and untied the double knot. As the bag fell down, there stood Theo, his hands tightly cuffed behind his back. The crowd gasped and, more often than not, stood dumbfounded and silent. They were simply too astonished to clap, too confused to cheer. How on earth could two men switch places like that in just a matter of seconds? How had Houdini escaped? Who had tied Theo up inside the bag? The stunned crowd would stare at Theo and Houdini and then silently walk away.

"What are we doing wrong?" Houdini asked Theo one afternoon. They had been performing their new trick for a few weeks, and no one had really taken notice. Houdini had been certain that the Metamorphosis trick would bring them instant fame. To make matters worse, Houdini misunderstood the crowds' silences. He thought that meant they were bored or unimpressed.

"Perhaps we need a new venue," Theo suggested. "Coney Island, maybe?"

Houdini's eyes lit up. Coney Island was a small island just a ferry ride away from New York City. It was dedicated entirely to entertainment and contained a resort, three amusement parks, and several white, sandy beaches. It was packed with all sorts of performers who did their acts anywhere from street corners to 2000-seat halls. Houdini had often thought about Coney Island, but he'd never been certain that his act was quite ready. But now he felt ready.

"Let's go tomorrow," Houdini responded confidently.

It didn't take long for the Brothers Houdini to find work. Once again, they found themselves in a dime museum, but this time it was in the midst of one of the amusement parks. There was endless energy and excitement, and for a change, the crowds cheered the Metamorphosis act instead of walking away frowning and scratching their heads. The act began creating such a stir that reporters began taking notice, and brief mentions of the Brothers Houdini began popping up in the New York papers.

In between shows—they were still performing fifteen to twenty a day sometimes—the brothers enjoyed strolling around the parks and catching the acts of other entertainers. In particular, Houdini insisted on seeing the other Coney Island magicians. Competitive and refusing to be second best, Houdini would watch other magic shows, taking notes and returning again and again to observe his competition. If there was even a shred of doubt in his mind about how a trick was done, Houdini could not stand it. Often, he would stay up all night thinking about a trick and reading magicians' books until he figured it out.

But Houdini also enjoyed watching other kinds of entertainers just for fun. Dancers, singers, clowns, musicians—these were the types of shows where he could just relax and not pay too much attention or worry about missing something. Certainly, these were not the kinds of shows where he felt compelled to return again and again for any reason.

Until one afternoon.

Houdini sat with his brother, half dozing and half watching a clown juggling eggs while running around in circles. It had been a long day, and the small tent where the performance was taking place was warm. As the clown exited the stage to bored applause, three young women entered. Billed as "The Floral Sisters," the women took the stage and began their song and dance routine. There was nothing particularly overwhelming about the talent of the three girls (who were, in fact, not sisters). But as Houdini watched the show with mild interest, he found that he could not take his eyes off the smallest performer. She was the most beautiful girl Houdini had ever seen. With huge blue eyes and curly blonde hair, she was barely five feet tall, making her look more like a child than the eighteen-year old that she was. In Houdini's eyes, she was like a delicate angel.

Houdini returned the next afternoon. And the next. Finally, he got up enough nerve to invite her to come and see The Brothers Houdini show.

"Perhaps," he said shyly, "we can take a walk along the boardwalk afterward."

The young woman, Bess, accepted with a smile. She was intrigued by this handsome young man about her age who claimed to be a magician. Bess had never met a magician before, and she had certainly never been asked out on a date by one. For his part, Houdini planned to impress and amaze Bess with his flawless show. But things didn't quite work out as planned.

When Houdini saw Bess sitting right up front in the very first row of seats, he was a nervous wreck. He was usually calm and full of self-assurance during a performance, but now his mind wandered and his hands shook. One of the very first tricks involved "disappearing ink," a bottle of which sat on a low table directly in front of Bess. In his confusion and nervousness, Houdini knocked over the bottle, and ink spilled all over Bess's dress, ruining it. Bess did not seem particularly upset, but Houdini was horrified.

Houdini insisted on replacing the dress, even though Bess claimed it was not that important. In great shame, Houdini visited Bess's home that evening so that he could have the ruined dress in order to replace it exactly. Bess's mother met him at the door with a glare. She already disliked this Houdini character for a number of reasons. For one thing, he was a magician, and she believed magic was evil. For another thing, Houdini was Jewish, and she thought Jews were evil too. But worst of all, he was interested in her daughter.

"You will not be seeing Bess again," she said shortly as she handed him the dress.

"Yes, ma'am," Houdini said sadly as he bowed politely.

"When you return, just leave the new dress at the front door. Do not come here again trying to see my daughter."

Houdini just nodded, turned around, and ran home.

Because Houdini gave most of his earnings to his mother, he had no money to buy a new dress. However, his mother took pity on him and agreed to make the dress for Bess. It took nearly a week. Every night, Houdini would pace back and forth by his mother as she sewed, wringing his hands and worrying. He really wanted to see Bess again, but he knew her mother would not allow it. It seemed so unfair. And, after all, he was twenty and Bess was eighteen. Weren't they old enough to do what they wanted to do?

Finally, the evening came for Houdini to drop off the dress. As instructed, he left the package at the door and turned to leave. Just then, the door opened. There stood Bess with a funny smile on her face.

"Weren't you even going to ring the doorbell?" Bess asked.

"Your mother . . ." Houdini began.

"My mother isn't here," Bess replied, looking directly at Houdini.

Houdini grinned and offered her his arm. "Well, then. Shall we go for that walk along the boardwalk?"

They took the quick ferry ride to Coney Island, where they spent the evening talking, laughing, and wandering through the carnival lights. As the night grew later and later, Bess began to worry about what she would say to her mother.

"I'm going to be in a lot of trouble," she said, shaking her head. "Both of my parents told me I was not to see you again."

Houdini's face clouded over. He was silent for a while as they walked on, hand in hand. Suddenly, he blurted out, "If you were my wife, they wouldn't dare punish you!"

Bess stopped and stared at Houdini in shock. "Harry . . . what are you saying?"

CHAPTER 4

When Houdini didn't answer Bess's question right away, Bess was more to the point.

"Harry, are you asking me to *marry* you?"

Houdini responded by grinning and grabbing Bess's hand. At that very moment, they were passing by a store that sold second-hand jewelry and cheap rings. Houdini pulled Bess through the door.

"Shall we see if they have any wedding bands that fit?" Houdini asked. He was still smiling, but Bess could tell he was serious. In her mind, Bess knew that it was crazy to marry someone she had known for only a week. But her heart told her otherwise. Without a word, she followed Houdini to the ring counter. Two bands were found that were a perfect fit. Unfortunately, Houdini revealed that he had only one dollar to his name. Bess ended up buying her own ring.

Harry's ring would have to wait.

Next, the two dashed to the office of the Coney Island Justice of the Peace. Around midnight on June 22nd, 1894, twenty-year-old Harry Houdini and eighteen-year-old Bess Rahner were married. Hardly believing it themselves, they rushed home to tell their families. Bess knew that her parents would be surprised and certainly upset at first, but she was not prepared for her mother's outrage.

"You *WHAT*?" Bess's mother, Mrs. Rahner, shouted while Mr. Rahner stood near the door shaking his head.

"But Mother, we love each other," Bess said helplessly.

"Out!" screamed Mrs. Rahner, pointing to the door that Mr. Rahner now held open. "I never want to see you or speak to you again. You have married an evil man, and now neither you nor your . . . your . . . evil magician husband is welcome in this house."

Bess stood staring at her mother. She turned to her father for help, but he wouldn't even look at her. Slowly, Bess and Harry walked out the door. And before slamming the door behind her daughter, Mrs. Rahner repeated her words: "I will never speak to you again!"

It was a promise she would keep for twelve years.

Harry's mother, on the other hand, loved Bess instantly. Mrs. Weiss was delighted that her son had found such a pretty and polite wife. And as cramped and poor as the Weiss household was, Mrs. Weiss welcomed her new daughter-in-law into it. She even sewed new clothes for Bess and gave her some of her own since Bess had been thrown out without a dime or even a change of clothes.

And within the week, Houdini had decided to also welcome his new wife into his magic act. He wasn't happy with the idea of Bess continuing to sing and dance for strangers out on Coney Island. He wanted to keep a closer eye on her. In addition, always the ambitious performer, he felt that a husband-and-wife team would attract more interest than two brothers. Bess was happy with the new plan, but now Houdini would have to break the news to his brother, Theo.

Luckily, Theo had already been thinking about striking out on his own as a magician, so he was not upset with his brother's decision. His only demand was that Houdini repay him for the Metamorphosis trunk, a demand that Houdini was happy to fulfill as soon as he earned the money.

The same evening that he told Theo of his new plans, Houdini asked Bess to accompany him up to a small attic room in the apartment. He motioned for her to be quiet as they tiptoed up the stairs.

"But what are we doing, Harry?" Bess asked.

"You'll see," Harry said mysteriously.

As Bess walked into the room, she could see the Metamorphosis trunk in the dim candlelight.

"What's your trunk doing up here?" she asked.

"Well," Harry said, "I want you to start doing this trick with me next week. And so . . ." Here Houdini sighed heavily and lowered his voice to the quietest whisper. "I must show you how it's done."

Bess simply nodded.

"You must understand something," Houdini said gravely. "You and Theo are the only ones who know. This is my greatest secret."

Hours later and well past midnight, Harry and Bess crept back downstairs. But Harry's plans for the night were not over yet. Tapping on Theo's door, Harry asked him to join Bess and himself. Into the warm, windy evening, Harry led his wife and brother to a deserted park where a little bridge crossed a dark creek. Heavy clouds swept by the full moon as Harry clasped hands with Bess and Theo.

"Bess, Theo, raise your hands to heaven and swear you will both be true to me. Never betray me in any way, so help you God."

Solemnly, Bess and Theo promised Houdini

that they would never betray him—never reveal how he performed his tricks. If Houdini's young wife had not been aware of it before, she now knew just how serious her husband was about his career, his magic, and his secrets.

In the early 1900s, the tour that every performer longed to be on was called "vaudeville." When a performer was on the vaudeville circuit, he or she performed nearly every night of the week and made very good money. Vaudeville shows were held in theaters, not in circus tents or dime museums. But, most importantly, there was always the chance to become famous. This was because vaudeville shows were made up of four or five acts ranging from unknown performers to the superstars of the day. If you got on the vaudeville circuit, you could be assured of a packed house nearly all the time. Regardless of how unknown you might be, people would always buy tickets to see the stars.

Harry Houdini longed desperately to become a vaudeville performer. Again and again, he would assure Bess that he was going to be world-famous as soon as he got his big break. Houdini understood that working the dives was the first step to getting noticed by the vaudeville agents. But Houdini was growing restless and impatient working the dime museums. He and Bess had begun traveling to other cities to perform in new museums, but the pay remained low, and the crowds were often no more impressed with Houdini than they were with a nine-toed cat or a bearded lady. When would his big break come?

"Maybe we're playing for the wrong kind of crowd," Houdini said to Bess one night after a long day of seventeen shows. "Maybe we should try the circuses for a while."

Bess just nodded, though she was not at all sure about performing in a circus. Granted, the work was steadier, and people bought tickets for seats instead of just walking by, but she had heard about the circus life. It could be dirty, dangerous, and very hard. In terms of show business, it was not considered any better than the bars or dime museums.

Houdini saw the worried expression on Bess's face. He threw his arms around her and held her tight. Just as he had always been with his mother, Houdini could not bear to see Bess sad or disappointed.

"Everything will be all right," he promised. "Our fame and fortune is just around the corner. Wait and see."

The only light on the road came from the occasional flashes of lightning as Houdini and Bess struggled through a horrible downpour. In addition to their suitcases, they were hauling the Metamorphosis trunk, which was packed with all the other gear for their shows. Both Bess and Houdini were soaked to the skin, and mud covered their feet.

"Are we lost, Harry?" Bess shouted over the storm.

"I don't know how we could be," Houdini shouted back. "This is the only road from the train station. Mr. Welsh said they'd be right down this road." Bess and Houdini were in a remote part of Pennsylvania in the middle of the night, looking for the Welsh Brothers' Circus. Mr. Welsh had sent them a brief note saying that he might hire them if they could join the circus in Pennsylvania. There was no guarantee of work, but he'd look them over and decide.

Suddenly, a gruff voice barked out from the pitch blackness: "Is that the Houdinis?"

"Yes!"

A tall man appeared without a word and pulled them both into what looked at first like a cave. But as Bess and Houdini's eyes adjusted to the dim lantern light, they could see that they were in an old truck. The truck had been turned into living quarters for several people.

"Well, what do you want to do?" the gruff voice barked again. It was Mr. Welsh.

"Any kind of work at all, sir," Houdini replied politely.

Welsh glared at Houdini and his wife for several seconds. "All right," he finally said, "here's the deal. The wife will do song and dance and mind-reading tricks. You, Houdini, will do your magic plus some handcuff tricks and anything else we need you to do."

Houdini was apprehensive about the mind-reading. He and Bess had never done that before. But they were desperate. "Yes, sir. That sounds fine," Houdini agreed.

"Twenty-five dollars a week for sixteen weeks. A place to live and food to eat. Take it or leave it," was Welsh's first and final offer.

It was not very good money, but Houdini had no choice. He took it. After signing an agreement, Houdini and Bess were shown to their "room." It was no more than a corner of the truck separated from the other "rooms" by a thin, dirty curtain. The furnishings in the room consisted of a tiny cot barely big enough for one person. Still soaking wet, Bess collapsed on the cot and burst into tears. Houdini did his best to console her until she fell asleep. Then he stayed up most of the night making notes about how he and Bess would do their acts.

"Hey you, Houdini! Get out here and put some makeup on!"

Houdini woke with a jump. The sun was already high in the sky. He scrambled through the curtain to see what Welsh wanted.

"Look, I'm gonna need you to dress up as the 'Wild Man of Java' for our first show today.

Our regular guy is sick. It's advertised, and the audience will raise hell if we don't have him."

"Yes, sir," Houdini answered cheerfully. "But what exactly do I . . ."

"Oh, just the typical stuff," Welsh interrupted. "Act like a savage. We'll throw you raw meat and you growl and run around on all fours."

Houdini nodded and headed toward the costume tent. It wasn't that Houdini had no pride. He knew when to say no. But he never turned down the chance to at least try a new kind of performance. More than anything, he was curious about how audiences would react. What made them laugh? What frightened them? What intrigued them? In the long run, it was this desire and curiosity that, in a big part, led him to success. So Houdini messed up his hair; painted black, red, and blue streaks on his cheeks; and dressed in a piece of torn burlap.

Pulled out into the crowd in a sturdy cage, Houdini, now the Wild Man, growled and howled and made threatening lunges at anyone who approached the cage. He tore at raw meat and even ate it. The crowd loved it. To taunt the Wild Man, they threw cigarettes and cigars into the cage. Houdini never smoked cigarettes or drank alcohol, but when the show was over, he collected all the cigarettes and handed them out to his coworkers. Houdini had never considered playing a savage in a traveling circus, but he was a hit. Welsh replaced the former Wild Man with Houdini and raised Houdini's weekly pay by five dollars.

Something else that neither Houdini nor Bess had ever considered doing in their act was mind-reading, but now they would have to learn the tricks of that trade too. And quickly. Welsh gave them only two days to prepare. As always, Houdini read books and discussed the finer points of the trick with other circus actors who had seen the mind-reading act performed.

"There's nothing to it," San Kitchi, the sword swallower, said to Houdini. "When we get to a new town, visit the graveyard or read the death notices. Jot down the names of people who have recently died and how they died. Then have your wife claim that she's reading the mind of someone who's just lost somebody. When she says the name and how they died, everyone will be amazed."

Houdini nodded, but he wasn't sure he felt quite right about doing that. Kitchi saw his apprehension.

"You can also just eavesdrop on people in town," Kitchi said with a shrug. "Walk around for a couple hours, and you can get all sorts of information. But wear a disguise."

Two nights later in a small town in Ohio,

Bess sat in a chair in front of the circus audience. The lamplight was dimmed as she pretended to go into a trance. As she drifted into her trance state, Houdini would prepare the audience.

"Tonight, here before you is a woman with talents far beyond explanation or understanding! Even now, she is preparing to read a complete stranger's mind."

With that, Bess would begin to sway and moan and slowly begin to speak:

"Someone here . . . tonight . . . is . . . is . . ." Bess would begin in a low voice. The audience would sit absolutely still, waiting breathlessly for her next words. "Someone is planning a trip to . . . hmmmm . . . to . . . California!"

There would be a gasp and a stirring in the crowd. "That's me!" a startled voice would call out.

Then, for the next ten minutes or more, Bess would provide all the details of this stranger's trip while the stranger and the audience sat stunned—details overheard by Mr. Houdini just that afternoon as he waited for lunch in the local cafe, wearing a fake moustache and a pair of glasses.

Sixteen weeks with the Welsh Brothers' Circus went by quickly. Although the circus life was never easy, Bess and Houdini learned a great deal and made some good friends. In particular, Houdini befriended Kitchi. Kitchi revealed to Houdini how he swallowed swords. He also taught Houdini how to swallow small objects (such as keys or coins) and then bring them back up from his stomach, a skill that Houdini would find useful in later years. And, most importantly, he shared a very old but rarely-practiced trick called the "Needle Trick." In this trick, it appeared that Kitchi swallowed ten sewing needles and then a piece of thread. After waiting a couple of minutes to let everything "digest," Kitchi would slowly pull the thread from his mouth—with all ten needles attached!

But when their time with the circus came to an end, Houdini and Bess found themselves stranded in St. Louis with no work and very little money. In keeping his promise to his father, Houdini had faithfully sent his mother nearly all of his pay every week. Now the Houdinis were reduced to shivering in an unheated and filthy hotel room in the dead of winter.

Then one day, the money ran out completely.

"Harry, what are we going to do?" Bess asked, her voice full of worry.

Harry had been trying, in vain, to find work for a few weeks, but nobody had any use for an unknown magician. He even applied to work as a locksmith, but there were no jobs available. Finally, in utter despair, Houdini walked through the doors of the St. Louis newspaper and offered to sell them the secrets of all his magic tricks for only twenty dollars. Certainly, they could not turn down such an intriguing and valuable story. But they did.

Nobody was even interested in Houdini's most precious secrets. He had, it seemed, finally hit rock bottom.

CHAPTER 5

Worse than the traveling circuses, lower than the dives, and on the very bottom rung of the performance ladder were the traveling medicine shows. A "medicine show" had very little to do with a show and even less to do with medicine. It was, basically, a dishonest way to get people to spend money on something worthless. And in the spring of 1898, the Houdinis, desperate for work, joined Dr. Hill's California Concert Company—a rundown medicine show that wasn't even from California.

Here's how medicine shows worked. The owner, usually referred to as a "doctor" even though he had no medical knowledge, traveled from small town to small town trying to sell his "wonder potion." The wonder potion often came in a bottle, and the doctor typically claimed that it could cure anything from baldness to heart failure. In reality, the potion was nothing more than a little cheap whiskey mixed with water.

In order to sell the potion, the doctor needed to draw a crowd. That's where the "show" part came in. Dancers, singers, magicians and the like were hired to perform briefly. As soon as a crowd gathered, the show was over and the doctor appeared, shouting enthusiastically about his miraculous potion. Unbelievably, dozens of people would buy the phony medicine. This, literally, kept the show on the road.

Day after day, Houdini stood on small-town street corners and performed card tricks, coin tricks, and handcuff escapes for handfuls of people. It was a depressing time for Houdini, and for the first time in his life, he seriously considered giving up the dream of being a magician. Still, he carried on, trying to focus his energies on getting better and not on giving up.

In particular, Houdini was focusing on his handcuff escapes. He believed that he was one of the best escape artists around, and he was sure that his talents would and should amaze any crowd. Two, three, sometimes even four pairs of cuffs were locked to Houdini's arms. After being cuffed, he would disappear for only a few minutes behind a screen that blocked him from the crowd and then reappear—completely free!

But nobody seemed even vaguely impressed by his handcuff escapes. People were much more interested in the card tricks or even in Bess's phony mind-reading show.

"I don't understand it," Houdini complained to Bess after a crowd didn't even applaud for his handcuff act. "It's the most difficult trick I perform, and no one cares!"

Another performer who was standing nearby overheard Houdini. "If you don't mind me saying this," the man said politely, "I believe the audiences think your handcuffs are fixed. I've heard some people say so."

"Fixed?" Houdini asked.

"Yes," the man continued, "they just assume that you have fixed the cuffs so that you can simply shake them off easily when you disappear behind your screen."

Houdini was shocked. "But these are real handcuffs! They are regulation police cuffs!"

"That may be," the man said gently, "but the audience doesn't know that. No policeman put them on you—you did it yourself."

Suddenly, Houdini had a brainstorm.

"I know what to do!" he said grabbing Bess. "I know how to get famous!"

Bess had heard this before, but something was different this time. Houdini's eyes blazed. He picked her up and spun her around.

"First thing tomorrow morning," he

announced excitedly, "I'm headed to the police station to get locked up!"

"I can get out of any handcuffs you want to put on me," Houdini said bravely to the big, burly chief of police in Chicago.

"That's great," the chief said without even looking up from his morning paperwork.

"So go ahead." Houdini stuck out his arms to be handcuffed. The chief of police continued to ignore him. *This isn't working*, Houdini thought desperately. He had spent his and Bess's last few dollars on their train ride into Chicago from the small Illinois town where they had been performing with the medicine show. *What do I have to do to get this guy to lock me up?* Houdini decided to take a risk.

"Nah, I bet you don't have anything strong enough to hold me," he said with a mocking laugh. "I guess that's the problem. I dare you to even try."

That did it—a challenge! The chief of police slowly lifted his head. "All right, you little . . ." He shook his head at Houdini and then yelled into the back room for some of his officers to come and lock up this annoying magician.

"Feel free to use your strongest cuffs," Houdini said cheerfully. "And I'd be glad to be thrown into one of your jail cells, too. I'll have no problem breaking out."

The officers laughed as they shackled Houdini. What a fool he was! Then one of the officers decided to make an even bigger fool out of this strange little man. He asked a messenger to get some reporters from the *Chicago Tribune* to come in and cover the event. It would make a pretty funny article. As the reporters were arriving, the police were escorting Houdini into a padlocked cell.

"See you soon," Houdini said merrily as the jail door slammed shut. The entire group of officers and reporters burst into laughter. Then they walked down the hall to have a cup of coffee, still snickering and snorting. They figured they'd let this poor sap out in an hour or two when he'd learned his lesson.

In fewer than ten minutes, Houdini trotted down the hall to join the group for coffee. The chief of police's face went pale.

"But . . . but . . . this isn't possible!" the chief sputtered.

"He must have had keys and picks hidden in his clothes," the reporters insisted. "Anyone could do that."

Now Houdini grew angry. More than anything, he hated to be accused of using an easy and unimaginative way of escaping handcuffs. "I did not have anything of the kind." He paused, glaring at the group, a million thoughts racing through his head. "I'll tell you what," Houdini finally said. "I'll strip naked, you can search me, and I'll still escape."

A dead silence filled the room. The officers looked at their chief. The chief glared at Houdini. The reporters all tapped their pencils. The clock on the wall ticked.

"All right, then," the chief finally said through clenched teeth. "Let's do it."

Now this was a story! The reporters rushed back to the paper to get photographers. The police officers quickly gathered up the cuffs and chains again. Proving that he had nothing to hide, Houdini stripped right in the middle of the police department. Then, once again, he was bound with handcuffs and chains and thrown into a cell.

"All I ask is that I am left alone to do my escape," Houdini explained to reporters who wanted to see how he did it and remained standing outside the jail cell. "Professional secrets. You understand."

The policemen and reporters left. Within minutes, Houdini came bounding down the hallway stark naked with the chains and cuffs in his hands. The reporters wasted no time dashing back to write up this story.

"Hey what's your name, anyway?" one of the reporters asked as he headed for the door.

"Harry Houdini," Houdini answered proudly, "King of Handcuffs."

Fame did not suddenly blossom overnight. Houdini had made a splash in a big city, but as soon as the waves settled, he was back to being unknown. However, Houdini had learned something tremendously important—people love to be challenged. As Houdini and Bess resumed working in a dime museum in Chicago, Houdini added a new twist to the show. He let it be known that he would pay fifty dollars (a lot of money in 1899!) to anyone who brought in a pair of handcuffs that he could not escape from. This accomplished two things: it proved that he was a real escape artist who was not using "fixed" cuffs, and it created a buzz about his talent. Of course, this was long before radio or television, so Houdini put up posters around the city announcing his challenge. The posters featured a picture of him covered in handcuffs and very little else. Soon, hundreds of people were flocking to Houdini's shows.

Occasionally, the challenge would backfire. Once, a man brought a pair of handcuffs that had been tampered with. He had filled the keyhole with cement and also bent the metal near the keyhole. Houdini struggled with the cuffs for nearly an hour behind the curtain. The audience began to boo and finally left.

"You give up?" the man shouted.

"These cuffs have been tampered with," Houdini said angrily as he walked around the curtain to face his challenger, still wearing the cuffs.

"Don't matter," the man replied shortly. "You said you could break out of any cuffs. That was the deal. Now pay me my money."

Houdini learned the hard way to check handcuffs and chains before putting them on. That night, the cuffs had to be sawed off and Houdini was suddenly fifty dollars poorer and flat broke again.

"Well, that's it. My career is finished," Houdini said gloomily to Bess. "No one wants to see a King of Handcuffs who is no longer king."

"But Harry, it was unfair. And hardly anyone was left to see you have to pay that man," Bess said.

"It doesn't matter. Word will get around, and people won't forget. I'm done for . . . doomed!" Houdini said dramatically.

However, the next day, the shows were packed again. Apparently, no one really cared. And Houdini learned another important lesson: just as one story in a big newspaper does not ensure fame, one mistake does not ensure failure.

Several weeks later, a man with a heavy German accent approached Houdini and Bess after a show. He had some very heavy handcuffs from Germany that he wanted to challenge

Houdini with, but first he wanted to have coffee with Houdini and Bess.

"How can I be sure that you are not fixing the cuffs when you examine them onstage?" the man asked.

Houdini thought this was a strange question, but he was polite. "Sir, I would be glad to examine them right now in front of you if you'd prefer."

The man watched Houdini closely and then, satisfied, took his cuffs back. He then spent another hour or more chatting with Houdini and Bess about their lives as performers, their act, and their dreams. He seemed unusually curious, even nosey, Houdini thought. But Houdini remained polite and answered the man's questions as well as he could.

The next afternoon, the man with the German accent showed up with his cuffs. Houdini escaped from them easily, puzzled as to why the man had made such a big deal about them. Then he and Bess went on with the rest of the show—the Metamorphosis, card and coin tricks, and the Needle Trick, the stunt that Houdini had learned from the sword swallower. When the show was over, the man stood across from Houdini with a smile on his face. As Houdini was packing up, the man finally walked over and stuck out his hand.

"Mr. Houdini, I don't believe I've even introduced myself. I'm Martin Beck."

For only a moment, Houdini was speechless. *Martin Beck!* Houdini certainly knew the name. Beck managed a chain of vaudeville theaters from Chicago to San Francisco known as the Orpheum Theaters—the fanciest and highest-paying theaters in the United States. Beck was a star maker.

"Mr. Beck, I . . . I—" Houdini fumbled for words.

"I'll be in touch," Beck said, shaking Houdini's hand firmly.

Two days later, a telegram arrived. "I'd like you and Bess to open the show in Omaha, Nebraska, next week on March 26, 1899, for sixty dollars. I'll come and see the show. If all goes well, I will probably make you a proposition for all next season."

Houdini, nearly in tears, grabbed Bess and shouted, "We did it! It's finally happening!" Then, at the bottom of the telegram, Houdini wrote in large handwriting: "This letter changed my whole life's journey."

The first thing Martin Beck did after watching Houdini's show in Omaha was to tell him what was wrong with it.

"Look, kid, you have to drop all those card and coin and disappearing scarves tricks. No one cares about that stuff, and you're wearing the audience out with too many little things. Stick with the Metamorphosis, the Needle Trick, and the handcuff escapes. That's all. Got it?"

Houdini nodded.

And I'm signing you up for the next twelve months. We'll start you at ninety a week and move up from there if things work out."

Ninety dollars a week! That was three times the money Houdini had ever earned in one week. All he could do was nod and thank Mr. Beck.

Houdini had finally gotten his big break, and he wasn't going to blow it. Although vaudeville required only two shows a day (as opposed to the fifteen to twenty in the dime museums), Houdini worked nonstop perfecting his show, thinking up new techniques, and reviewing every night's show over and over again in his mind. He slept barely four hours a night, and Bess would often have to remind him to eat.

The audiences loved him. And it wasn't just because of his amazing tricks. There was something about Houdini that mesmerized people. Martin Beck had seen it right away. Houdini was not a big man, but he had a way of taking over the stage when he walked out on it. His voice was mysterious, and his eyes were piercing. His utter confidence in himself and in what he was doing was enough to keep the audience's undivided attention. And when it was all over, Houdini was friendly and down-to-earth, often inviting strangers backstage to chat.

From Omaha to San Francisco, Houdini was a sensation. Although he was not the headliner of the show, he was moving up quickly. When he reached San Francisco, he rushed to the police station and repeated his jail-cell escape. Because he was becoming well-known as a vaudeville performer, the police station was jam-packed with newspaper reporters. Houdini made the front page of the *San Francisco Examiner*. Back in Chicago, Martin Beck received a copy of the paper and boosted Houdini's pay to over one hundred and twenty-five dollars a week. Houdini bought Bess a fur coat and sent his mother more money than she had ever seen in her life.

As the year's tour neared its end, Martin Beck sent a letter instructing Houdini and Bess to pack their trunks and bid farewell to America—it was time to conquer Europe. Beck assured Houdini that he would encounter even greater success in Europe since no magician had ever performed handcuff escapes before. Houdini would be the first.

Although Houdini was excited about Europe, the trip there was a nightmare for him. In 1900, the only way to get to Europe was by steamship, and the trip across the choppy Atlantic took nearly two weeks. Standing on the deck with Bess, Houdini waved goodbye to his dear mother as the big ship pulled out of the New York harbor and headed toward the open sea. Having never been on a ship before, Houdini couldn't wait to watch the land disappear and feel the ocean surround him. He hugged Bess and breathed a deep breath of salt air and then . . . suddenly, Houdini didn't feel all that great. Within minutes, he was green. For eleven days and ten nights, Houdini remained terribly sick. The man who could escape anything could not escape his own seasickness. Bess later swore that Houdini was in so much agony that she was afraid he'd throw himself overboard. As a result, she tied him to his bunk. Apparently, Bess Houdini knew how to tie the kind of knots her husband could not untie.

But Houdini survived the crossing. After a couple days of recovery in their hotel room in London, Harry and Bess headed over to the famous Alhambra Theater to meet with the manager and discuss the shows that Martin Beck had lined up. Houdini strode into the manager's office, full of confidence, his hand extended for a handshake. But the manager just gave him an irritated look.

"Who the hell are you?" he asked.

"Harry Houdini, King of Handcuffs," Houdini responded with a smile.

"Never heard of you," the manager said.

"But I'm booked to play here for the next six—"

"Booked to play *here*? I hardly think so," the manager snapped. "This is the Alhambra. We only book the best."

"But Mr. Martin Beck assured me that—"

The manager cut Houdini off one last time. "Now look, I don't know anything about any King of Handcuffs. We had some handcuff escape guy a couple years ago who was horrible and we won't make that same mistake again. Now if you don't mind, I'm very busy."

With that, he pointed to the door. Bess and Houdini had no choice but to leave. They stood in the foggy morning air of the West End of London, 3,470 miles from home and suddenly unemployed.

CHAPTER 6

"**M**artin Beck is fired!" Houdini shouted to no one in particular as he and Bess stood outside the Alhambra Theater. "I never want to see him again!"

Bess shook her head. "But Harry, there must be a misunderstanding. Mr. Beck would not send us all the way over here without any work waiting for us. Something's wrong."

"Something's wrong, all right," Houdini fumed. "I've been paying him fifteen percent of everything I earn for over a year now, and now this happens. I'm looking for a new agent."

Houdini and Bess sat down on the steps of the Alhambra, trying to think. They certainly had enough money to return to the United States, but Houdini was in no hurry to get back onboard a ship. And here they were in the middle of London, surrounded by theaters and opportunities. There *had* to be a way to get the ball rolling.

"I'm going back inside," Houdini finally said with a frown as he headed back to the door of the Alhambra Theater. "I'm not giving up this easily."

The theater manager was none too pleased to see Houdini back in his office again, but before the manager could protest, Houdini was already talking.

"Sir, I am sorry that there has been a misunderstanding, but I can assure you that my escape act will be unlike any that you . . ."

"Look," the manager said angrily, rising to his feet, "for the last time, no one is interested in your act. Everyone knows that escapes from handcuffs are phony. The so-called escape artist we had here last year was nothing but a con artist with fixed cuffs."

"But, sir," Houdini cried out quickly, "my escapes are entirely authentic! Allow me to prove it to you."

"Prove it? How?" the manager asked suspiciously.

"Take me to Scotland Yard and have them lock me up," Houdini replied without skipping a beat. Scotland Yard was the London prison— a prison well-known throughout Europe for its state-of-the-art methods of both punishing and restraining criminals. The theater manager laughed out loud.

"You're telling me that you think you could escape from the Yard?"

"That's exactly what I'm telling you," Houdini answered calmly. "And I don't just think it—I know it."

The manager stared at Houdini. He certainly had to give this little American magician credit for having a lot of nerve. "I'll make you a deal, then," the manager finally said. "If you can manage to escape from Scotland Yard, I will give you your own show at the Alhambra. But if you cannot escape, I had better never see you again."

"It's a deal," Houdini said with a broad smile.

What actually happened at Scotland Yard that morning may be part fact and part fiction. No one knows for sure since the reports of it mostly came from Houdini himself, and Houdini was known to spice up stories about himself in order to help his own publicity. But in any event, this is the story that remains. . . .

After much laughter by the London police, they agreed to handcuff Houdini and imprison him as he had requested. But at the last minute, the police superintendent decided to handcuff Houdini with Houdini's arms stretched around a wide pillar instead of behind his back. This way, it would be impossible for Houdini to move his arms or even see his hands. It was how the most dangerous criminals were locked up. Houdini, showing no fear, agreed to it.

The superintendent placed four pairs of heavy regulation handcuffs on Houdini's arms. Then, the superintendent clamped them shut, stretching Houdini's arms tightly around the pillar.

"I'll be back for you in a few hours," he said as he turned to leave the room and walk down the hallway.

"But wait!" yelled Houdini. "I'll go with you!" The sound of metal falling to the floor startled the superintendent, but the sight of Houdini, free from the cuffs, startled him even more. It had taken fewer than five seconds. Had Houdini known of a flaw in the design of English cuffs? Had he really escaped in a matter of seconds? Regardless of whether there was fiction involved in the retelling of his escape, it was a fact that Houdini was hired for his own show at the Alhambra at the astounding salary of $300 a week—a sum equal to nearly ten times that in today's money.

The news of Houdini's escape from Scotland Yard swept through London like a fire out of control. Houdini's first show at the Alhambra was standing room only, and Houdini did not let the curious crowd down. He amazed and baffled them. Although Martin Beck had messed up Houdini's European bookings, he had been right about one thing—no one had ever seen an escape artist like Houdini. And so the Alhambra booked

Houdini for a week solid, and then another week, and then another, until Houdini had been playing sold-out shows at the famous Alhambra Theater for nearly four months. Not bad for an unknown magician who had arrived in London without one booking.

About midway through his run at the Alhambra, Houdini felt that it was time to add something new to his show. At this point, his show consisted of handcuff challenges and escapes, the Metamorphosis, the Needle Trick, and an assortment of illusions. Many people returned to see Houdini's show again and again, and he realized that he needed something exciting and unusual to keep them returning. What Houdini decided to add was certainly unusual.

A couple of years earlier, while touring in Nova Scotia, Houdini had been invited to visit a hospital for criminally insane patients. This may seem like an odd place to visit, but Houdini was always curious to learn about how people were restrained in extreme circumstances. As a doctor led Houdini down the long hallways of the hospital, Houdini peeked through cell windows at patients. Suddenly, he stopped dead in his tracks. Inside this particular cell was a young man struggling to free himself from a straitjacket.

Houdini had never seen anything like it. He rushed home and immediately made notes about what he'd seen: "I saw a maniac struggling on the canvas padded floor, rolling about and straining each and every muscle in a vain attempt to free himself . . . I noted that were he able to dislocate his arm at the shoulder joint, he would have been able to free his arms . . . this was the first time I saw a straitjacket, and it left so vivid an impression on my mind that I hardly slept that night."

Indeed, Houdini had been so fascinated with the straitjacket that he decided to add an escape from it to his show. And to add a twist, Houdini decided to do the escapes right in front of the audience, not behind a screen as he did with handcuff escapes. It was a hit. Audiences were stunned to watch Houdini fall on the floor, wriggle and squirm, dislocate his own shoulder, free an arm, readjust his shoulder, and rip the straitjacket off. Houdini had always strongly denied trickery when it came to escapes, and now his straitjacket routine proved it.

However, one night, one of the show's regular escapes went terribly wrong—an escape that did, in fact, involve a little trickery.

Bess had continued to do the Metamorphosis act with Houdini. Houdini was the one bound, placed in a tied sack, and then locked inside the trunk. Bess would then pull a curtain around the trunk, something that audiences expected in magic performances. Curtains or screens were often used briefly to protect the magicians' secrets. The curtains did not lessen the mystery; on the contrary, they heightened the audiences' curiosity.

Once the curtain had been pulled around the trunk, Bess would disappear behind the curtain, clap her hands three times, and, within mere seconds, would have changed places with Houdini. Curtain or no curtain, it was unbelievable that the two could have switched places in only seconds. Furthermore, the act was popular because Houdini always encouraged audience members to check out the trunk and locks for themselves. Try as they might, audience members could not find anything wrong with the locks, and the trunk was clearly solid wood. How on earth did Houdini escape, and how did Bess get inside?

Here was the secret: built into the trunk was an expertly hidden sliding door. It was impossible to see, and since it was on the inside of the trunk, it was even less likely to be noticed. Most people from the audience were more concerned with the locks and the solid construction of the outside of the trunk. And as the trunk was sealed shut with Houdini inside, and as audience members were double-checking the padlocks, Houdini was already escaping. The cuffs? These were no problem for him to undo in seconds. The tied bag? What the audience didn't know was that the bottom of the bag (hidden from view) was slit open. All Houdini had to do was pull the bag over his head. Next, he quietly pulled open the sliding door as Bess, behind the curtain, was clapping her hands three times. Quickly, Bess crawled inside the trunk and slid the door shut.

Houdini would then push the curtain aside with a loud "Behold!" As the audience was cheering, amazed at the sight of Houdini before them, Bess was slipping into the bag and snapping on the handcuffs. Now all that was left for Houdini to do was to unlock the trunk and reveal Bess inside. But one night, the master key for all the locks on the trunk had accidentally been left in the dressing room five floors above the stage. Houdini tried to stall for time as he sent his forgetful assistant rushing upstairs for the key. But Bess became alarmed when the trunk was not unlocked. Unlike Houdini, she was not able to remove the handcuffs. Though she, of course, knew about the hidden door, her hands were not free to open it—and it only opened from the inside. She began yelling for help and kicking the inside of the trunk. The audience, thinking it was part of the show, laughed and clapped, but soon they became concerned.

Houdini tried to remain calm, but he knew Bess was in real danger—there was only enough air in the trunk to last eight minutes. *Where was the assistant with the key?* Bess's shouts became more frantic, and Houdini rushed offstage to look for help. Returning with an axe, Houdini was just about to chop into the trunk when the key arrived. When the trunk was finally unlocked, Bess had passed out. Houdini carried her offstage in his arms. Although Bess had had a terrible scare, she recovered quickly.

Following this near-tragedy, the London press became obsessed with trying to figure out how the Metamorphosis worked. How was it that Houdini could escape, but his wife, even in a life-threatening situation, could not? The more that was written about this event, the more famous Houdini became. And because Houdini was such a wizard with his own publicity, some still believe that the whole event was planned, and that it was just a way for Houdini to get more attention.

Whether the trick was phony or real did not matter. Houdini was suddenly swamped with attention. Every major theater across Europe, and even into Russia, contacted Houdini, begging him to perform. And the amount of money that many of these theaters were willing to pay Houdini was truly astounding. As expected, Houdini happily accepted all invitations to perform at high-paying theaters, and he and Bess found themselves traveling and performing non-stop for the next four years.

The very first stop Houdini made in any new city was a visit to the local police station.

His escapes from prison cells and handcuffs were becoming legendary. More often than not, the police were not nearly as thrilled as the spectators when Houdini escaped their best restraints. After all, it was humiliating and a little embarrassing for the police to be quickly outdone by this little magician. So as time went by, the police escapes got more and more difficult.

In Germany, the police used five different kinds of handcuffs, thumbscrews, finger locks, and chains. Houdini's mouth was taped shut, he was stripped, and his arms were yanked tightly behind his back. All this before being tossed into a padlocked cell. The press, waiting outside, looked at their watches. Before the minute hand had passed six minutes, Houdini was free. The German police grumbled and shook their heads.

In Russia, Houdini became fascinated with the idea of escaping from a Siberian Transport Cell. This was a solid steel carriage that was used to carry the worst prisoners to exile in Siberia, and it was considered escape-proof. Houdini, upon seeing it, described it as "a large safe on wheels." One key opened the carriage to allow the prisoner to enter. But the only key that would unlock the carriage was hundreds of miles away in a remote Siberian prison. As always, Houdini was stripped, cuffed, chained and thrown into the back of the metal carriage. Minutes ticked by— ten, twenty, thirty . . . the Russian police folded their arms and smiled smugly. But forty-five minutes later, Houdini, sweating and bruised, emerged from the back of the carriage. He had done the impossible.

The Russian police were furious! They angrily informed the press that the story could not be printed in the papers. They refused to believe that Houdini had outdone them, and they simply insisted that he had cheated in some way. In fact, to this day, no one has figured out how Houdini could possibly have escaped the Transport Cell. It remains one of his greatest mysteries.

But even though the Russian police forced the press to keep the escape quiet, news of Houdini's escape spread quickly by word of mouth throughout Moscow. Within hours, Houdini had become more than a talented magician—he had become a hero. Certainly, Houdini's escapes were entertaining and fun to watch, but in countries like Russia and Germany in the early 1900s, the idea of escape and outwitting the police gave people hope. In these countries, many people lived under what was known as a "police state." This meant that the government gave the police the right to control the way people lived. As a result, the police were often terribly strict and cruel, forcing citizens to obey unfair laws and ridiculous rules. People who resisted even slightly were brutally punished. It had gotten to the point where many felt there was no escape from the police state—

then Houdini came along. "People over here fear the police so much," Houdini later wrote, "and I am the first man that has ever dared them."

However, Houdini and Bess did not remain in Russia for long. In addition to being a police state, Russia was promoting hatred and violence toward Jews. The leader of Russia at the time, Czar Nicholas II, went so far as to authorize the military and the police to terrorize and kill Russian Jews. Decades before Hitler, Nicholas II was already on a mission to wipe out the Jewish population in his country. Although Houdini had somehow managed to hide the fact that he was Jewish during his brief time in Russia, he never felt safe. Both Houdini and Bess breathed a great sigh of relief when they finally returned to England.

Now it was time to go home. The Houdinis had been in Europe for nearly five years, and they were terribly homesick for the United States. In particular, Houdini missed his mother. He had regularly sent her large sums of money and exchanged letters, but he longed to see her and take care of her in person. But before leaving Europe, Houdini had one more task.

On a cold December morning, Houdini boarded a train to the tiny town of Blois in France. This was where his hero, the magician Jean Houdin, was buried. Houdini wanted to pay his respects and visit the Houdin family, who still lived in Blois. Upon arriving in the little town, Houdini bought a large wreath of flowers to place on the grave. Then he wandered down a cobblestone street to the Houdin house and knocked on the door.

"I'm sorry, but Madame Houdin does not wish to see you," came the reply from the butler.

"But I told you to tell her that it is Harry Houdini," Houdini responded.

"I did," the butler answered in an irritated tone. "She has no idea who you are, and she has asked you to leave."

"No idea who I am!?" Houdini asked in disbelief. By now, Houdini was famous throughout Europe. And it is no understatement to say that his ego had gotten fairly large. It was truly impossible for Houdini to believe that someone had not heard of him—particularly someone related to a magician. "But I am the Great Houdini!"

"That may be," the butler concluded, "but Madame does not know you. Good day." And with that, Houdini had the door slammed in his face.

Stunned, Houdini walked in a daze to the graveyard where Houdin was buried. When he found Houdin's tombstone, he kneeled by the grave for a full half hour with his head bowed. Then he gently placed the wreath of flowers against the stone and headed back to the train station.

Houdini would never say much about his visit to the Houdin house and how he was abruptly turned away. But he would not forget it. Buried deep inside, his anger and pain would grow quietly for nearly seven years. Eventually, he would get his revenge.

CHAPTER 7

Handcuffs are Houdini-proof!
These are handcuffs no mortal man could pick!
Let's see the Self-Liberator get out of this steel trap!

Houdini and Bess were already packed for their trip back to the United States when a London newspaper, the *Daily Illustrated Mirror*, ran a front-page article about a locksmith who had spent five years designing the most escape-proof pair of handcuffs ever. The locksmith had devoted five years to one goal: dethroning the Handcuff King. Houdini sat staring at a picture the paper had printed of the big, ugly cuffs.

"I have to do it," Houdini said to Bess. "It's the biggest challenge anyone's ever presented to me."

Bess agreed. She had known as soon as she had seen the newspaper headline that their trip home would have to be postponed for another few days.

"And since the *Mirror* is involved, they'll give it all sorts of publicity," Houdini said with a gleam in his eye. "I'll bet I sell out the Hippodrome."

Houdini was right. The London Hippodrome, the largest theater in England, sold more than four thousand tickets in only a few hours. Houdini would not even be performing his regular show—just the escape from the handcuffs. Even so, ticket prices were high, but no one complained. It was the show of the year.

Two days later, at three in the afternoon, Houdini walked onstage and simply shouted, "I am ready!" The audience of thousands gave him a standing ovation. A *Mirror* reporter snapped the heavy cuffs on, and a band began to play. As he always did when performing handcuff escapes, Houdini stepped behind a screen out of the view of the audience in order to work in private. People settled into their seats to wait. And the band continued to play. It may be hard today to imagine how audiences could be entertained by simply sitting and staring at a screen while listening to music, but the people of that era loved it. As the minutes ticked by, the tension grew as audience members imagined how Houdini must be struggling. Would he be able to do it? What was he doing to try to escape?

After nearly forty minutes, Houdini appeared from behind the screen. Audience members gasped—he was still handcuffed! Houdini was drenched with sweat, and the collar of his coat had torn open. Blood trickled from both hands.

"May I have a pillow?" Houdini asked, his voice cracking. "My knees hurt." The reporter placed a pillow behind the screen, and Houdini disappeared. And the band played. Another twenty minutes passed, and Houdini appeared again still cuffed, sweating, and bleeding.

"Could you please remove the cuffs for a second so that I may take my coat off?" he asked weakly.

"I am sorry, Mr. Houdini," the newspaper man said, "but I cannot unlock those cuffs unless you admit that you are unable to escape from them."

Now Houdini grew angry. Admit defeat? Never! Twisting awkwardly, Houdini was able to pull a small knife out of a pocket. In a fury of jerks and turns, Houdini literally cut himself out of his coat. The audience erupted into five minutes of nonstop cheering as Houdini returned behind the screen. Ten minutes later, he emerged, waving the opened handcuffs high over his head.

"A mighty roar of gladness went up," the *Mirror* reported. It was Houdini's European farewell performance. But everyone knew he would return some day—he was a mega-superstar.

Although Houdini had hired a new agent in Europe, Martin Beck had always remained in touch. He had apologized again and again for messing up Houdini's European shows, but Houdini remained distant. Clearly, Beck did not want to be on bad terms with a star. So when Beck heard that Houdini was finally returning to the United States after years of astounding success in Europe, Beck sent an encouraging letter. He assured Houdini that his success would follow him back across the Atlantic. Beck promised a hero's welcome, complete with brass bands, cheering crowds, and excited reporters.

But when Bess and Houdini arrived in the New York harbor and walked down the gangplank, there was no band. There was no crowd, and not one reporter was present. In fact, no one even recognized the Great Houdini. When he filled out the paperwork necessary for returning from overseas, the clerk had no idea that "Houdini" was a household name in other parts of the world.

Although Houdini's ego was bruised, he didn't dwell on the absence of a hero's welcome. Obviously, the crowds were more interested in seeing him perform. So Houdini wasted no time in marching right into the offices of the biggest theaters in New York City and naming his price. It was a price, however, that no theater was willing to pay.

"I'm sorry, Mr. Harooni, but we'd never sell enough tickets to be able to pay you that much," one theater manager explained.

"It's '*Houdini*,'" Houdini snarled, "and I've sold out every theater in Europe for years."

"Well, yes, certainly we've heard of you over here, but there just isn't enough interest in your act to give you a show of your own yet. Perhaps we could let you open a show for a song and dance company from—"

"NO!" Houdini shouted and stormed out of the theater office. *How could this be?* Houdini fumed as he slammed the theater door. *All these years of work and fame, and I can't even get my own show in my home country!*

Houdini took a long walk around the city, trying to calm down and sort things out. He had faced difficult challenges before, but this was just too much. He had already paid his dues. He refused to pay them again. Later that evening, he sat across from Bess and told her what he had decided.

"We must return to Europe," Houdini said solemnly.

"But, Harry, we've only just arrived back home! Don't get discouraged so easily."

Houdini took his wife's hands in his own and looked straight into her eyes. "This has nothing to do with being discouraged. I have my pride. I have achieved stardom, and I will not start over again. Not here, not anywhere."

Bess nodded—she understood and agreed without words. She and her husband of, now, ten years were unusually close. Houdini shared every thought, every dream, and every worry with Bess, and Bess did the same. A marriage that had seemed ill-thought-out and reckless at first had turned out wonderfully.

Houdini sighed, and then a look of angry determination covered his face. "I will not return to the United States until the theater owners here *beg* me to come back and do my show. That's a promise."

So Houdini and Bess had barely unpacked their trunks when they had to start planning for the long journey back across the Atlantic. But before leaving, Houdini longed to do something special for his mother. For years, Houdini had been faithfully sending his mother more than enough money to make her life quite comfortable. Once, he even paid to bring her to Europe. When she arrived, he took her to her home town in Hungary and threw a huge party for her. He had even bought her a very expensive dress for her to wear for the occasion. But now he wanted to do even more.

Houdini's mother still lived in the family's old rundown apartment. Now that only

Houdini's sister still lived with their mother, there was more room; but the apartment was old, drafty, and in a bad part of town. So before leaving, Houdini decided to buy his mother a home. Since Houdini's mother spoke German, he bought a house in a German-speaking neighborhood. And since his mother had had to live in cramped quarters for so many years, he bought something a little bigger—four stories with twenty-seven rooms, to be exact.

Houdini and Bess would also live in the house when they were home in New York, but that would not turn out to be very often. Houdini's favorite room would always be his study—a large room filled with the hundreds and hundreds of books he collected throughout his life. Bess was glad to finally have a bright, shiny kitchen to work in, and Houdini's mother was just glad to be able to live her older years in a beautiful home. Houdini, now an exceedingly wealthy man, paid the $25,000 for the house in cash.

"I'll need twenty-four volunteers for my next act," Houdini shouted out to a packed theater back in London. Twenty-four hands shot up. Houdini invited the volunteers up on the stage. As they gathered around him, Houdini showed them a bowl with twenty-four sewing needles in it.

"I will now show you how much stronger the mind is than the body," Houdini announced to the audience and volunteers. "What you are about to witness is a skill I learned from an old Hindu man. Therefore, I refer to this next act as the Hindu Needle Trick."

With that, Houdini picked up one of the needles and jabbed it into his cheek. The audience gasped. Then Houdini picked out another needle and handed it to the first volunteer. "Please feel free to push this needle into any place on my head except my eyes."

One by one, all the volunteers stuck needles into Houdini's face. At first they were hesitant, but when they saw that Houdini neither bled nor seemed to be in pain, they began jabbing them into his nose, lips, and even ears. Finally, all twenty-four needles stuck out of Houdini's face. As he smiled and spoke, the needles moved and quivered. The audience was not sure whether to be horrified or fascinated.

"And now, I feel the need for a snack," Houdini said casually. With that, he began pulling the needles out of his face and popping them into his mouth. The audience could actually hear the metal crunching and grinding as he seemed to be chewing them up. When he was finished eating all the needles, he swallowed a long piece of thread. He followed this with a long drink of water.

"Please," Houdini said to one of the volunteers, "check to make sure I have swallowed all the needles." The volunteer peered into Houdini's mouth and nodded. There were no needles.

"Perhaps, though," Houdini continued, "you might find a piece of thread in my mouth." Again, the volunteer looked in and found the end of the thread.

"Does everyone not agree that a needle needs to be threaded?" Houdini asked the audience. The audience, mesmerized, nodded slowly.

"Well, then, pull the thread out, please," Houdini instructed the volunteer. Slowly, the thread was pulled out. And every single needle was neatly threaded along it with exact spacing. By the time the entire thread was pulled from Houdini's mouth, it was twenty-four feet long. The audience sat stunned for nearly a minute before bursting into cheers.

This was, at the time, one of Houdini's most puzzling tricks. How he managed to endure having twenty-four needles stuck into his face has never been totally figured out. However, it has been suggested that Houdini planted his "volunteers" in the audience for this part of the trick. They weren't volunteers at all—they were assistants who made it look as though they were sticking needles in Houdini's face when, in fact, it was just an illusion created by, perhaps, lighting, heavy makeup, and fake needles.

The swallowing and threading of the needles was a simple trick—that is, simple for Houdini.

Houdini did place all twenty-four needles in his mouth. As mentioned, they were probably not real needles with sharp points, but simply blunt-tipped pieces of metal. After Houdini pretended to be chewing them up and swallowing them, he took that long drink of water. But there was more than water in the cup.

First Houdini quickly spit out, into the cup, all the needles and the piece of thread he had pretended to swallow. Meanwhile, floating around in the cup was a tightly-wound packet of twenty-four needles that had been pre-threaded. Houdini tucked the packet into his cheek, moving it around so that the end of the thread would be visible to the "volunteer." Then, the volunteer simply pulled the thread and needles out as Houdini allowed the packet to unwind in his mouth.

"Now look, Mr. Houdini, we can't allow you to risk your life like that," a London police officer said as he shook his head.

"But it's no risk. I know what I'm doing," Houdini explained.

"Seems mighty dangerous to me," the officer said.

"Well, that's the point," Houdini replied. "No one would want to see it if it didn't *seem* dangerous. But you must believe me—I know how to escape without injury."

The officer took some more convincing, but he finally gave in. "Okay, friend. It's your funeral," he said with a shrug.

The next afternoon, a London square was packed with thousands of people. Every one of them stared skyward. Nine stories above the crowd, hanging upside down with a rope tied around his feet, Houdini was swinging back and forth in a strong breeze. Wrapped tightly around him was a straitjacket. Everyone had come to see if he could escape from it in midair. What if the wind picked up even more? What if the rope around his feet became loose as he struggled? What if he passed out from hanging upside down for too long? The crowd watched tensely.

Twisting like a madman, Houdini fought wildly with the straitjacket. The rope holding him bounced, and the wind nearly blew him into the building's brick wall. But bit by bit, Houdini loosened his restraint. Finally, in one dramatic movement, Houdini ripped the straitjacket over his head and sent it flying down to the crowd below. The thousands of spectators erupted in a roar of approval.

A week later in Paris, Houdini had a coffin carried onstage.

"There is only enough oxygen when the coffin is sealed shut to last fifteen minutes," he shouted. "If I cannot escape, this will not only have served as a stage prop—it will serve as my final resting place."

There was something about seeing Houdini climb into the coffin that both terrified and fascinated the audience. No one had ever seen anyone do something like that. It made the idea that Houdini could die trying to escape all the more vivid. Adding to the terror was the fact that Houdini invited volunteers from the audience to come up and quickly hammer the coffin shut with heavy nails. As always, a curtain was pulled around the coffin. Audience members could hear Houdini banging away inside the coffin, and they could only imagine how horrifying it must be to be sealed within a casket.

Minutes ticked by. Suddenly the banging slowed down. Then it stopped altogether. Had Houdini died? A nervous murmur rumbled through the audience. It had been more than twelve minutes . . . then thirteen . . . then . . .

"Behold! I have escaped death yet again!" Houdini jumped out from behind the curtain and took a deep bow as two thousand people gave a standing ovation.

Of course, it was no accident that Houdini had suddenly added frightening and bizarre acts to his show. As always, he had a plan. Back in the United States, news of Houdini's act was spreading. In particular, pictures of Houdini hanging upside down, bound in a straitjacket, one hundred feet up in the air, or smiling with a face full of needles, or climbing into a coffin caught everyone's attention. While his act before had been exciting, pictures of it were not. Suddenly, everyone in the United States was eager to read about this Harry Houdini and to see pictures of his most recent escape from death.

Before long, telegrams from major U.S. theaters were being delivered daily to Houdini. They all said something like this: "We would love to book you for a week or more of your own shows. Will pay you top dollar. Please contact us immediately."

Houdini smiled. "Now that's more like it," he said quietly.

CHAPTER 8

If Houdini had been determined to become a star in Europe, he was twice as determined to become a star in his own country. Although he had, as always, been terribly seasick on the trip home, Houdini wasted no time as soon as he was back on dry land. The very first thing he did was to take a train to Washington, D.C. He had an appointment with prison cell #2 on Murderer's Row of the South Wing of the United States Jail. It had already been widely publicized in the New York and Washington papers that Harry Houdini was the best escape artist who had ever lived. Now he would attempt the ultimate prison escape.

Cell #2 was infamous. A narrow walkway led deep into a brick wall. Within the wall was the prison cell. The lock of the heavy iron door was not even on the door—it had been installed around the corner from the cell, entirely out of reach. And to add to the cell's mystery, a number of notorious murderers had been held there until their execution. One of the most recent had been Charles Guiteau, the man who shot and killed President Garfield.

Houdini was tossed into this cell, naked and handcuffed and chained as usual. His clothes were locked in a different cell at the other end of Murderer's Row. Eight other murderous prisoners sat in cells around him. As the jail warden would later write: "Mr. Houdini, in about two minutes, managed to escape from the cell and then broke into the cell in which his clothing was locked up."

But it didn't end there. Houdini decided to have a little fun with the other prisoners. One by one, he unlocked all eight cells, led the prisoners out and locked them back up in different cells. The warden did not quite see the humor in this. After all, these were killers Houdini was dealing with! Typically, Houdini had no fear of the potential danger in this escapade. And the tidal wave of publicity that followed had made it all worthwhile.

Several days later, Houdini was in the midst of planning his next spectacle when Bess suddenly became terribly sick. When it looked as though Bess might not recover, she asked to see her mother. It had been twelve years since Bess's mother had sworn that she would never speak to her daughter again. So far, she had kept her promise. Houdini certainly must have dreaded the idea of seeing his hateful mother-in-law, but he rushed to her house anyway.

At first, Mrs. Rahner would not even look at Houdini. She firmly refused to return to Houdini's house to see her sick daughter.

"All right," Houdini said slowly, trying to control his anger. "Do what you want, but I am not leaving your house until you agree to come and see your daughter." Then, in a more pleading tone, Houdini added, "Mrs. Rahner, she's very sick."

Bess's mother looked at Houdini then, and she saw that there were tears in his eyes that he was trying hard to force back. Without a word, she ran for her coat and hat. As soon as she and Bess saw each other, they both burst into tears, hugging one another and apologizing for all the pain they had put each other through. Mrs. Rahner helped nurse Bess back to health, and through it all, she was touched by how devoted and caring Houdini was toward her daughter. Over time, Bess's mother would become proud of Houdini and realize just how wrong she had been about him. And years later, as an old woman, she would be welcomed into Bess and Houdini's big house, living there in luxury until the day she died.

Houdini had come to a new decision about his career. Even though his shows would still continue to feature illusions and interesting tricks, he wanted most to be known as the *greatest* escape artist alive. And he wanted those escapes to become more and more dangerous. In his nearly fifteen years of performing, Houdini had learned a lot, but one thing stood out. It was something he had realized even as a child, watching the tightrope walker in the circus—people loved nothing more than watching a performer risk his life.

And so, a series of risky escapes began.

In November 1907, Houdini gathered reporters in Detroit, Michigan, to watch him jump off a bridge and into the frozen Detroit River. This was one of his first river jumps, so he invited only the press. He figured the publicity alone would be worth the jump. A large hole had been cut in the ice for Houdini to jump through. He was handcuffed and wearing almost nothing when he leaped from the Belle Isle Bridge. What happened next has often been questioned, but Houdini always stood by his story.

The plan was for Houdini to return to the surface through the ice hole after he had freed himself from his handcuffs. But the current was too strong on that day, and Houdini was quickly swept downstream. He was able to remove the cuffs quickly, but the solid ice kept him from being able to emerge. Thinking quickly, Houdini began swimming against the current, looking for the hole. He knew that a small space always exists between ice and water, so every so often, he would breathe the air trapped in that space.

But back on the Belle Isle Bridge, reporters assumed the worst. Houdini had instructed an assistant to drop a rope through the hole if he hadn't appeared in three minutes. A rope was dropped, but no Houdini. Ten minutes later, reporters sent newsboys into the streets of Detroit. "Houdini drowned! Houdini drowned!" they shouted. Bess had stayed at the hotel, too afraid to watch her husband jump. When she heard the shouts below, she buried her face in her hands. But at that very moment, Houdini burst through the ice hole, shivering and shaken, but nonetheless triumphant.

That night, every seat in the Detroit Theater was taken. The audience did not consider that being nearly naked in freezing water for that long would have been physically impossible for Houdini. Nor did they focus on the fact that most of the Detroit River was not even covered in ice on that particular afternoon! The audience wanted to believe Houdini had cheated death, and so they did. However, it's worth noting that in later accounts of this miraculous frozen-river escape, Houdini changed the date to later in the winter when the river was, in fact, frozen over.

Then, while playing a week of shows in Boston one fall, Houdini set his mind on one of his most bizarre escapes on record. One morning, a fisherman working off the coast of Cape Cod caught an extremely odd creature in his net. Even seasoned fishermen who had been working on fishing boats for fifty years had never seen anything like it. It weighed more than 1,600 pounds and looked like something from a bad nightmare—either a cross between a giant turtle and a bloated octopus or a whale with a massive shell and tentacles. When the fisherman brought the creature ashore, it caused a sensation. The newspapers simply referred to it as a "What-is-it?"

Immediately, Houdini saw an opportunity. Gathering his assistants, he arranged to have the sea monster carted through the streets of Boston. Houdini stood on the cart near the What-is-it, shouting out his plans for the evening. Throngs of people stood dumbfounded when they heard what Houdini was saying, but they were not too stunned to dash out and buy tickets for that night's show.

That afternoon, two taxidermists worked quickly to open up the What-is-it, clean it out, and cover it with a very strong substance called arsenic in order to keep it from rotting. Then,

metal clamps were installed all along the opening, and hooks for locks were attached to the
clamps. As the workers neared the end of their
job, Houdini walked in to inspect the creature.

"Ah, perfect," he said with a smile. "Escaping
from the belly of a giant sea monster has never
been done before."

"Not likely to ever happen again," one of the
workers mumbled sarcastically.

"Exactly," replied Houdini with a wink.

But what Houdini thought would be a simple, though truly strange, escape did not turn out
as planned. As soon as he settled inside the What-
is-it at that night's performance, he knew he was
in trouble. The fumes from the arsenic instantly
made him dizzy and sick to his stomach. In a rare
fit of panic, Houdini began to kick the inside of
the beast, hoping it would simply break open.
But instead, it rolled over and began to smother
him. In just the nick of time, the assistants
managed to turn the beast over, and Houdini
popped out. Although the audience realized that
Houdini had required some help in this escape,
they were still impressed when he jumped out of
the creature. After all, he'd been locked in the
gut of a monster.

Around this time, Houdini had been increas-
ing his river jumps. He realized that crowds were
particularly thrilled and frightened by the sight
of a chained and handcuffed man being thrown

underwater. The possibility of death by drowning always drew the most attention. Now Houdini wanted a way to bring that thrill to the stage. But he'd have to make it even more daring and more dangerous if he wanted to keep the crowds interested.

Finally, Houdini came up with a terrifying idea. It combined the risk of being trapped in a very small space with the danger of drowning. In Houdini's day, milk was delivered to stores and restaurants in thick metal cans about the size of a medium trash can. Houdini found one that was just big enough for him to squeeze into, with his knees tucked against his chest and his head bowed when the lid was tightened. Into this can, Houdini would have assistants pour water until it reached the brim. Then Houdini would climb inside, sending water splashing onto the stage. Keeping his head above the rim of the can, Houdini would shout out to the audience:

"My assistants will now seal and lock the lid. Failure to escape will mean a death by drowning! I am a mortal man and can hold my breath for only so long. Please, hold your breath along with me!"

The lid was then clamped down and six padlocks clamped shut, with volunteers from the audience checking the locks to assure that they were real. The curtain was drawn around the milk can. What became known as "the world's largest stopwatch" was wheeled out onto the stage. As audience members held their breath, they watched the second hand sweep by. A theater of a thousand or more people was soundless. After thirty seconds or so, however, almost everyone began gasping for breath. Still the second hand kept moving. At a minute and a half, a police officer holding an axe stepped near the milk can. At two minutes, he raised it over his head. But at just under two and a half minutes, a soaking-wet Houdini bounded around the curtain, waving and smiling. The impossible had happened again.

But there was a secret to this "impossible" escape. Hidden several inches beneath the padlocked lid was a second lid. This lid was attached by small, smooth latches on the inside of the milk can. Nobody could see them. All Houdini had to do was hold his breath for a long time and then easily flip open the latches and crawl out.

Of all the unusual escapes that Houdini accomplished during his rise to stardom in the United States, there was only one that he vowed he would never repeat—being buried alive. Wanting to imitate a true burial, Houdini insisted on being buried six feet underground. As usual, he was handcuffed; but when the dirt began piling up on him, Houdini felt complete terror. He had finally gone too far. *I won't make it out!* Houdini thought as he clawed and kicked at the dirt. *It's too much . . . too heavy. . . .* It was the closest Houdini ever came to dying during an escape. Between his panic and the unexpected weight of the dirt, Houdini could not even figure out which way was up. Assistants grabbed their shovels and dug frantically. When they reached Houdini, he was bleeding and choking on dirt. "Never again," he whispered before collapsing.

"I want to do this," Houdini said to Bess at breakfast one morning. He was pointing to a picture in the newspaper. It was a strange picture that Bess couldn't quite make out. It looked like a giant bird.

"Do what?"

"I want to fly."

It was 1908, and the first airplanes, mostly designed by the Wright brothers, were being flown by daredevil pilots around the world. The airplanes were extremely fragile and were often compared to eggshells or paper bags. More often than not, the planes crashed and crumbled to bits. It was considered dangerous and even a little foolish to fly one of these early airplanes. And that, of course, was all Houdini needed to know.

"Can you imagine?" he asked. "Actually flying above the ground?" Houdini had that unmistakable fire in his eyes that Bess was all too familiar with. She saw it every time he decided to take on a new challenge.

"No," she said smiling, "but I can imagine that you'll know what it's like soon."

So Houdini bought an airplane for $5,000. It came complete with instructions on how to climb into the cockpit and how to turn the engine on and off. And that was it. At the time, there were only a few dozen pilots in the world, so any real training was years in the future. Houdini was on his own when it came to learning how to pilot one of these "eggshell" planes. He practiced running the plane down the road at a low speed several times. And then it was time for his first flight. It was not a pretty sight. That night, all Houdini wrote in his diary was, "I smashed the machine. Broke the propeller all to hell."

But give up after the first try? Not likely for Houdini! He immediately began looking for a new plane to buy. But now he wanted to add a little more to the challenge. It had become something of a race to be the first person to fly an airplane in a country. Planes had already been flown in North and South America and in Europe, so Houdini would have to find another country. After a little research, Houdini made up his mind. Within a month, Houdini had bought another plane, loaded it into a crate, and, along with Bess, boarded a ship bound for Australia.

The long trip to Australia was very hard on Houdini. The crossing took nearly a month, and Houdini was seasick the entire time. By the time the ship finally reached Australia, Houdini had lost twenty-eight pounds. According to Bess, he had eaten a grand total of fourteen meals the whole time. Also, his first grey hairs appeared during the trip. It took Houdini nearly a week to gain enough strength back to begin preparing for his flight. And there was no time to waste. Much to Houdini's annoyance, he discovered that a local mechanic named Banks had heard that Houdini was on his way to Australia with an airplane. Banks wanted to beat Houdini in the race to the sky. He had already ordered an airplane from America that had been delivered days before Houdini arrived.

Luckily for Houdini, the weather had been terrible all week, and Banks could not attempt a flight. But now both Banks and Houdini went to the airfield with their planes every morning at dawn, waiting for the winds to calm down and eyeing each other to see who would make the first move. Finally, Banks became impatient. He jumped into his fragile plane and revved the engine. Houdini let him go. An expert at sensing danger and bad timing, Houdini predicted that Banks was headed toward disaster. He was right. Banks zoomed across the field, and the little plane lifted up into the air. But almost immediately, a gust of wind slammed the plane to the ground, shattering it to pieces. Banks suffered only a black eye—his ego received the worst injury. To be considered a "first flight," the plane needed to remain in the air for at least two minutes. Banks had missed that requirement by a minute and fifty-five seconds.

Houdini waited. Finally, a morning arrived that was so still it was almost eerie. Houdini, Bess, and a small group of curious onlookers and press people rode out to the airfield. Putting on his flight goggles and a cap, Houdini prepared for takeoff. He tested the air for wind one last time and then took off across the grassy field. Suddenly, the little plane floated like a feather up into the air. The group below cheered as Houdini climbed up to more than two hundred feet. But when Houdini turned the plane, it met a sudden wind. Without warning, the engine died, and the plane began diving toward the ground. Just in time, Houdini restarted the engine and swooped back up, waving and smiling triumphantly. He remained in flight for more than three minutes. Houdini had won the race. He was the first person to ever fly a plane in Australia.

The press described Houdini's flight as "risky and death-defying"—something that Houdini was more than happy to agree with. But other members of the press suggested that he had intentionally turned off the engine in order to make the flight more dramatic. Houdini angrily denied any such trickery. He insisted that flying one of these eggshell airplanes was both terrifying and dangerous. It is interesting, then, to read his diary entry the night after his flight in Australia: "I was never in any fear and never in any danger. It was a wonderful thing!"

So, was Houdini fooling the world, or was he fooling himself?

CHAPTER 9

Houdini's favorite magicians were dead magicians. Why? Because a dead magician could not compete with Houdini. More than anything, Harry Houdini could not stand competing with another magician—or, rather, he could not stand being beaten by another magician. Even as a teenager running races in Central Park, Houdini viewed coming in second as losing. Now, as a grown man, Houdini refused to allow any other magicians to be better than he was at escapes or illusions.

Houdini succeeded in beating his competition in several very different ways. First of all, he worked exceedingly hard. It was not unusual for Houdini to stay up all night perfecting a new technique, and he ignored his own exhaustion time and again. He read everything about magic and performing that he could get his hands on, and he was fearless in trying new and dangerous tricks.

But Houdini also maintained his top-magician honors in not so admirable ways. As Houdini became world-famous, he made up his mind to go to any lengths to remain number one. And one of those lengths was to reveal other magicians' secrets. More than once, if Houdini noticed that audiences were becoming too thrilled with another magician's trick, Houdini would simply explain how it was done. After that, audiences were not as interested in the magician or his tricks.

Professional magicians, of course, considered this the worst kind of behavior. How dare Houdini destroy other magicians' careers just to help his own! Suddenly, Houdini was the focus of scorn and ridicule by other magicians of his day. He was called a bully, a liar, a cheater, and worse. Magicians who had long been jealous of Houdini's success were more than happy to jump on the bandwagon. At first, Houdini just laughed it off. In his mind, the uproar his actions had created only made him more famous. The more that other magicians called Houdini names, the more the public would flock to his shows to see the man who had stirred up so much anger.

But in time, the insults began to wear Houdini down. Little by little, Houdini grew bitter toward other magicians. In addition to this bitterness, Houdini still felt some anger toward the Houdin family. He had never forgotten or forgiven the rude treatment he had received when he had gone to visit the grave of Jean Robert-Houdin. It was, then, perhaps a combination of bitterness and anger that led Houdini to write a book about Houdin titled *The Unmasking of Robert-Houdin.*

It was not a kind book. For whatever reasons, Houdini gathered all the years of research he had done on his hero and put together a book that, basically, presented Houdin as a fake. According to Houdini, Jean Robert-Houdin stole all his tricks from other magicians and then tried to pass them off as his own. He was, Houdini continued, "an ignoramus in certain lines of conjuring." Worst of all, Houdini simply described the man whom he had once patterned his life after as "a rotten magician."

Other magicians, particularly those in Europe—since Houdin was French—were appalled. They could not begin to understand how Houdini could destroy the reputation of an icon, particularly an icon that Houdini had worshiped and even borrowed his name from. But Houdini was not intimidated. Rather than backing down or apologizing, Houdini headed straight into the eye of the storm, returning to Europe to do several months of shows. The bickering and anger of fellow magicians over *The Unmasking of Robert-Houdin* did not seem to keep the crowds away. If anything, they were more curious than ever about Houdini—and his book. Before long, Houdini was not only the top-selling performer in Europe; he also had a bestseller! It seemed that Houdini was on top of the world. Then, in an instant, everything came to a halt.

"Call a doctor! Something is wrong—Mr. Houdini has collapsed!"

At a party following a big show in Hamburg, Germany, Houdini had excused himself for a moment from a conversation with two members of the Danish royal family. He had suddenly remembered that he had been handed a telegram from the United States right before his show had started that evening. Assuming that it had to do with business, Houdini had tucked it in his back pocket to read after the show. Now, at the party, Houdini's eyes had quickly scanned the telegram, and his face went deathly pale. Then he slumped to the floor unconscious.

Bess ran to her husband's side. Kneeling on the floor next to him, she picked up the telegram and read it. It was from one of Houdini's brothers: *Harry, please come home right away. Mama has died.*

"My dear little mother. Poor Mama," Houdini was crying as he regained consciousness. Out of respect, the partygoers all left the room, leaving Bess alone with her grief-stricken husband. But Houdini was so overwhelmed that he couldn't even walk. Bess had to find Jim Collins, Houdini's favorite assistant, to help Houdini back to the hotel room. On the way to the room, Jim innocently asked, "Can't you do anything for your mother, Mr. Houdini?"

Houdini stared at Jim weakly. "Do anything? What do you mean?"

"You know—something to . . . to . . ." Jim stumbled over his words.

Houdini understood. Jim, like so many people of that era, truly believed that Harry Houdini could perform magic, that he really was a wizard possessed with strange and wonderful powers.

"No, Jim," Houdini said quietly. "This is the will of God. There is nothing anybody can do now."

The last time Houdini had seen his mother, she was waving farewell to Houdini and Bess as their ship was leaving the New York harbor for Europe, only a month earlier. Houdini, like many of the passengers, threw streamers of paper off the deck and toward the crowd waving goodbye. Houdini's mother had caught one end of a streamer as Houdini held the other end.

"Hold on! Hold on! Don't ever let go!" Houdini had shouted, laughing and waving at his mother. But as the ship pulled farther out, the streamer snapped in two. Now, back on the very same ship, headed this time to the United States, Houdini lay on his bunk remembering that morning, tears constantly running down his face. He had always been unusually close to his mother and admitted it easily. "I'm what is called a 'mother's boy,'" Houdini had always said of himself, and now that his mother was gone, he felt lost.

After his mother's funeral, Houdini canceled all of his appearances for nearly a month. His sorrow had made him truly ill, with a kidney disease, and doctors warned him not to return to work too quickly. Houdini agreed without any complaint. For the first time in his professional life, Houdini had no desire to perform. His only activity for some time was visiting his mother's grave. Bess did her best to console her husband, but there was little she could do to cheer him up. It would simply take time.

And in time, Houdini did return to Europe to perform all the shows he had had to cancel. But as he toured from city to city, to one sold-out show after another, his heart was just not in it. "I am working in a sort of mechanical way," Houdini wrote to his brother, Theo. "I feel so lonely that I don't know what to do properly, but am hoping that eventually I will have my burning tears run dry. . . . I try to scheme as in the past, but I seem to have lost all ambition." Suddenly, the need to outdo all other magicians at any cost seemed unimportant and even silly. Although Houdini would regain his ambition one day, his mother's death changed him. Bitter competitiveness and pettiness were replaced by better qualities. At nearly forty-two years old, Houdini was realizing what was truly valuable and important in this life.

"You must be joking, Mr. Houdini." A recruiting sergeant for the U.S. Army sat back in his chair and grinned at Houdini.

"I most certainly am not joking," Houdini responded. "I am ready to do my part for my country." World War I had broken out, and Houdini was ready to go to Germany and fight. Eager to do something for others instead of just for his own career, Houdini had rushed to the army recruitment center as soon as he had heard that war had been declared.

"Well, first of all," the recruiter said, shaking his head, "you're too old. And second of all, I'm sure your unusual talents are better suited to other areas."

Houdini sighed. But then he stared thoughtfully at the sergeant, as a new idea occurred to him. Maybe there was a different kind of way he could "serve" the army.

"Let me ask you this, then," Houdini finally said. "What if I entertain some of the troops for free?"

The sergeant nodded. "That would be great."

"And how about if I explain how to escape certain restraints," Houdini asked carefully. "I don't mind giving away a few of my secrets for the sake of the war effort," he concluded with a smile.

Within a very short time, Houdini was entertaining and teaching troops throughout the United States and Europe. One of his favorite tricks to perform for troops was called "The Miser's Dream"—a simple trick that many magicians still perform today. Houdini would walk over to soldiers and seemingly pull gold coins out of their pockets, ears, or off the tips of their noses. It was a quick illusion in which the coins were actually up Houdini's sleeves. With a simple flick of his wrist, the coin would quickly, hidden from the soldiers' view, pop into Houdini's hand. But Houdini added a new twist. After all the gold coins—worth five dollars each—had been gathered, he tossed them to the soldiers. By the end of his year of entertaining the troops, Houdini had given away more than seven thousand dollars of his own money.

And the "secrets" that Houdini gave away about escaping restraints weren't really secrets at all. Basically, Houdini explained that his escapes had always required two things: "My first task has been to conquer fear . . . it is necessary to preserve absolute serenity of spirit. If I grow panicky, I am lost. . . . My second secret has been to train my body, to make not one muscle or a group of muscles, but every muscle, a responsive worker . . . to make my fingers super fingers, and to train my toes to do the work of fingers." In the end, the great majority of Houdini's hand-cuff and restraint escapes had involved no more "magic" than concentration, strength, and special conditioning.

As time passed, Houdini's very physically demanding escapes began to wear him down. Through the years, he had suffered injuries as a result of the strain that many of his acts required. A burst blood vessel in his kidneys, a broken ankle, battered and bloodied hands, pulled mus-cles—all of these and more nagged at Houdini as he grew older. When his months of entertaining the troops came to an end, Houdini decided to give himself a bit of a break from such physical stunts. Besides needing to rest his body, Houdini continued to be depressed about his mother's death. He lacked the energy and enthusiasm required for death-defying escapes. Still, Houdini longed to stun and amaze his audiences. And in his heart, Houdini knew that he needed a new challenge to help pull him out of the slump he was in. Surely, there must be something astound-ing that he could do that did not require punish-ing his body. Houdini thought long and hard. And in the winter of 1917, he came up with a plan.

"People are more impressed by things that disappear than by things that suddenly appear out of nowhere," Houdini was explaining to Bess backstage at the 5,000-seat New York Hippodrome Theater. "Audiences assume that something that suddenly appears must have been there all along. But when something simply vanishes . . ." Here, Houdini grinned as he glanced out to the stage and the packed theater. "Well, nobody can figure it out."

"But, Harry, this is ridiculous," Bess said, trying to suppress a giggle.

"Yes, I know," Houdini responded, hiding a smirk. "That's what makes it great."

Houdini strode out onto the stage, waving and bowing to the applause. And before the applause had even begun to die down, out walked, or, rather, thundered, a 10,000-pound Asian elephant dressed in a lovely blue scarf.

"Ladies and gentlemen, please meet Jeannie!" Houdini shouted. As the crowd expressed shock at seeing an elephant onstage, Houdini had Jeannie stand up on her hind legs and kiss him with her trunk.

Next, a huge box on wheels was rolled out. "Yes, take a long last look at Jeannie," Houdini announced. "In the next few seconds, I shall make her disappear into thin air!"

With that, the elephant was led into the

box, and the door was shut. The box was turned around so that the audience could see all four sides.

"Even the elephant doesn't know how this is done," Houdini joked. Then, Houdini took a deep breath to add to the suspense. He clapped his hands loudly three times and threw open the door of the box. The elephant had vanished!

To this day, researchers and magicians argue about how Houdini pulled off such a gigantic disappearing act. But most believe that the elephant walked into another box that was pulled up directly behind the first box while Houdini told his joke and took his deep breath. Because the back of the stage was dark, because all eyes were on Houdini, and because it was done so quickly, no one saw the switch. But no matter how it was done, Houdini made headlines in all the New York City papers the next day. Slowly, Houdini began feeling his heavy depression slip away from him—a disappearing act infinitely more difficult than making a five-ton elephant vanish.

Meanwhile, Houdini began quietly supporting retired magicians who didn't have enough money to live on. Perhaps it was his way of making up for the poor behavior toward his fellow magicians a few years earlier. Perhaps, since he no longer had to support his mother, he simply wanted to help someone else. Whatever his reason, it was not something he bragged about or even spoke about. In fact, many of the magicians that Houdini sent money to were men he'd never even met.

Once, several years after Houdini had begun helping retired magicians, an elderly man walked up to Houdini after a show.

"So good to see you!" the old man said, shaking Houdini's hand heartily with both of his hands.

Houdini looked carefully at the old man. "I'm sorry, friend, but I'm afraid I don't know you."

"Don't know me?" the old man said in a surprised voice. "Why, you've been paying my rent for four years!"

"Well then," Houdini said with a smile as he put his arm around the old man's shoulders, "so good to see you, too."

CHAPTER 10

"**W**hy, Mr. Houdini? *Why?*" Reporters and photographers crowded around Harry Houdini, shouting questions. He had just announced that he would be quitting his stage shows.

"Why are you quitting show business?" a writer for a New York paper shouted above the rest.

"Quitting show business?" Houdini asked with an exaggerated look of horror on his face. "Whatever gave you that idea?"

"Well . . . *you* did," the reporter responded, confused.

"No, I said I was quitting my *stage* performances," Houdini explained. Then he looked around the room with a proud smile. "From this point on, I shall entertain my audiences by starring in movies instead."

It was 1919, and the thrill of movies was sweeping the nation. Ever since the very first film seventeen years earlier, audiences had been hooked. This first film, *The Great Train Robbery*, was in black and white, without sound, and barely ten minutes long. But that didn't matter. People were amazed by pictures that actually moved— they were more magical than magic itself.

Houdini had been keeping a close eye on the movies. It hadn't taken him long to realize that vaudeville and stage shows were on their way out. Already, he was seeing fewer people at his shows on the night that a new movie was premiering. Houdini was still a huge star, but he was amazed at how quickly the stars of the screen were closing in on his number-one status. True, Houdini was not as viciously competitive as he had been before his mother died, but he still wanted to be successful. And, as always, he loved a new challenge.

And so Houdini and Bess moved to Hollywood, California. They rented a bungalow in the hills and welcomed the change of pace and change of surroundings on the West Coast. Because he was already a star, it didn't take Houdini long to find a producer who was interested in featuring him in a film, or a "flicker," as they were often called in those days. Houdini drove a hard bargain when it came to his contract. He knew he was taking a risk by switching from stage performances to movies, so he wanted the money to be worth it—and it was. Houdini not only managed to persuade the movie company to pay him $1,500 a week—an unimaginable amount of money in 1919—but he also was assured *half* of the movie's profits.

From 1919 through 1922, Harry Houdini starred in a series of movies. And while all the films had different plots, they all featured the same theme: Houdini escaping, at the last minute, from some terrifying situation. Audiences were treated to many of the same escapes they had seen Houdini do on stage, or from bridges, for years. In *The Master Mystery*, Houdini played a heroic undercover agent who had to free himself from ropes and handcuffs before criminals killed him. Later on in the movie, the agent somehow found himself tangled up in a straitjacket. And in *The Man from Beyond*, Houdini played a man who came back to life after having been frozen for one hundred years in the Arctic. Needless to say, a scene involving an escape from a frozen river made its way into the movie.

Children, especially, loved Houdini's movies. They couldn't wait to see his escapes on the big screen and then come home and "play" Houdini, tying one another up and snapping on toy handcuffs. But adults were not as thrilled. First of all, the escapes were filmed, not real. Even in the early days, people were well aware of the tricks moviemakers could do with film. Everyone also knew that the "escapes" took place on sets, not on icy rivers or in the midst of dangerous criminals. There really wasn't any chance that Houdini might not escape, so how exciting was that?

But there was a second, more important reason why audiences never really warmed up to Houdini, the movie star. Simply put, he was a terrible actor. All of the energy and charisma that came across when Houdini was on stage disappeared when he stepped in front of a camera. He looked stiff and awkward. He overacted to the point that some audiences laughed out loud during what were supposed to be serious scenes. And worst of all, his romantic scenes with the leading ladies of the day were disasters. Directors suggested that Bess leave the set while Houdini filmed these scenes. Apparently, they sensed that Bess's presence made Houdini nervous. But Houdini would not allow that. After a handful of films and poor ticket sales, Houdini was let go from his expensive contract. Nobody wanted him in "flickers" anymore.

Next stop: The Houdini Picture Corporation.

"If no one will star me, I'll star myself," Houdini announced confidently to Bess one afternoon. "Of course, it will take a lot of money," he added, not so confidently. In fact, it took so much money for Houdini to start up his own film corporation that he had to borrow from friends and business associates. Houdini assured them that it was an excellent investment. After all, hadn't he been a success at everything he'd ever set his mind to?

However, at this time, all Houdini was successful at was putting out one disastrous film after another. Because of his stubborn insistence on remaining a movie star, the movie reviewers were even more critical of all his films. After an advance screening of one movie, a critic from *Variety* wrote: "Perhaps the renowned Houdini is fading. . . . There is only one escape in this movie, and that is a poorly staged affair showing the star free himself from a giant water mill . . . then Houdini waltzes around in a tuxedo and dress suit."

Only one of Houdini's movies drew noticeable attention. During the filming of *The Grim Game*, a truly dangerous stunt was scheduled. Houdini was to walk from one airplane's wing to another airplane's wing—while the planes were in midair! But in the middle of filming the risky walk, the two planes suddenly collided. Both planes came tumbling to the ground. Immediately, the press swarmed. Had Houdini been killed? Was he hurt badly? Actually, Houdini had not even been on the set that day. A stunt double had filled in for him, and aside from a broken arm, the double was fine.

But the collision had been caught on film. And Houdini had movie posters printed that announced in very large print: "Planes Collide in Midair!! Houdini Unhurt!!" Of course, the planes *did* collide. And Houdini was unhurt—since he hadn't even been there. But the public saw the posters and assumed that they would get to see some real film of Houdini truly risking his life. When the truth got out, moviegoers were not amused. Shortly thereafter, Houdini's very expensive experiment in making movies came to an abrupt end. Once again, it was time to try something new.

Houdini's films may not have been the brightest moments of his career, but his failure on the big screen did not seem to hurt his popularity as a stage performer. When reporters questioned Houdini about the fact that he had said he was quitting stage performing, Houdini just smiled. With a wink, he suggested that maybe he had exaggerated just a bit. In any event, when Houdini returned to the stage, he was in bigger demand than ever. Being a movie star, even a bad one, had brought Houdini even greater fame. Now he could demand $3,000 a week—more than many men earned in an entire year in 1922.

But Houdini was restless. And in the back of his mind, something had been bothering him for a number of years now. All across the United States, more and more people were being drawn into spiritualism. "Spiritualism" was based on the belief that certain people, called "mediums" or "spiritualists," had the ability to contact dead people and have conversations with them. These mediums would hold eerie, dimly-lit gatherings known as "séances," during which the medium would go into a trance and, supposedly, speak with ghosts and spirits.

These séances may seem harmless enough. But many people, heartbroken and desperate to contact a relative or friend who had died, would pay a lot of money to a medium to "speak" with their loved ones. World War I had claimed the lives of more than 50,000 American soldiers—all of them much too young to die. As a result, the popularity of spiritualism peaked in the 1920s. Everyone, it seemed, wanted to remain in contact with a son, husband, or friend who had been taken from the earthly realm too soon.

Houdini had been interested in spiritualism ever since he had been a boy. As a twelve-year-old, he had once paid a few cents to see a medium "speak" with the dead Abraham Lincoln. Lincoln had been something of a hero to the young Ehrich Weiss. Ehrich had read several books about him and knew more than most adults knew about the popular president. And, apparently, he knew more than the medium.

"Mr. Lincoln is speaking to me." The medium swayed back and forth, his eyes closed tightly as he worked in a trance. "He says he will answer your questions now."

The room, full of curious people, remained quiet. No one felt quite brave enough to speak to a dead president. But Ehrich was not afraid.

"Mr. Lincoln, what did you do immediately after your mother was buried?" Ehrich asked.

The medium paused. Surely this must have seemed like an odd question. But slowly he answered in what was, supposedly, Lincoln's voice: "I was very sad. I went to my room and would speak to no one for several days."

Ehrich knew that the first thing Lincoln did was to get a preacher to say a prayer over his mother's grave because Lincoln's father had not wanted to pay for a service. After the séance was over, Ehrich politely confronted the medium about this.

"Well, I guess you caught me," the fake medium laughed.

Ehrich wasn't angry, just disappointed. Like most people, he wanted to believe that it was possible to speak with spirits.

"But all mediums aren't like you, right?" Ehrich asked hopefully. "There are real ones that can speak to ghosts, aren't there?"

The medium laughed. "Not that I know of, sonny. We're all tricksters."

Houdini never forgot this. As a magician, he was in the business of fooling people. But there was a difference between fooling people and lying to them. It was particularly bad when the lying involved preying on people's longing to contact loved ones who had died. This was why Houdini had been uncomfortable having Bess "contact the dead" during her mind-reading days with the Welsh Brothers' Circus.

All of his life, however, Houdini remained fascinated by spiritualism. He read every book he could find on the topic. Whenever he got the chance, he went to séances. Although his better judgment told him not to, deep in his heart, he wanted to believe in spirits. And now, after the death of his beloved mother, Houdini hoped beyond hope that maybe, just maybe, there were real spiritualists out there. He desperately wanted to speak to his mother, if only to say goodbye— something he had never gotten to do.

"My wife and I have had six conversations with our dead son. I can assure you that her powers are real, Harry. Certainly, I would not lie about my wife's ability to contact our son's spirit." Houdini was taking an afternoon walk with his friend Sir Arthur Conan Doyle, the author of the famous Sherlock Holmes stories.

"But how?" Houdini asked. "How is that really possible?"

Conan Doyle smiled at Houdini. "Well, now, certainly *you* of all people understand how secret powers work."

Houdini looked at him. Conan Doyle was

entirely serious. "Oh, but you can't actually believe that the things I do in my show are anything more than simple tricks or illusions," Houdini said.

"You still won't admit it, will you?" Conan Doyle said, shaking his head. "I know how you escape that milk can. Clearly, you are able to transform your body into a form, like a ghost, that can move through wood and metal."

Houdini resisted the strong urge to burst into laughter right in his friend's face. Houdini knew that many people believed that he had special powers, but it surprised him that Conan Doyle, a wise and educated man, would believe so strongly in spiritualism and secret powers. Houdini and Conan Doyle had often disagreed about whether or not spirits were real.

"I'll tell you what," Conan Doyle said after he and Houdini had walked in silence for some time. "Why don't you and Bess come over this evening? We'll have a séance and see what spirits show up."

Houdini was reluctant, but he didn't want to offend Sir Arthur or Lady Conan Doyle. He agreed that he and Bess would come over just after dark, when the spirits, according to Conan Doyle, were the busiest . . . and the most talkative.

That evening, the Conan Doyles and the Houdinis sat around a candlelit table. Lady

Conan Doyle held a pencil in her hand and positioned it over a blank sheet of paper.

"When a spirit enters the room," Lady Conan Doyle explained, "he or she will guide my hand to write out his or her message to us."

Perhaps Houdini rolled his eyes in the dim room, but a small part of him still wanted to believe. The room was deathly quiet. Then, slowly, Lady Conan Doyle's hand began to move across the sheet of paper. At the very top, it drew a cross.

"It's your mother, Harry!" Lady Conan Doyle whispered. "She has come to speak to you." Then, Lady Conan Doyle's hand moved at lightning speed across page after page, filling the blank sheets with words from Mrs. Weiss to her son. Houdini sat utterly still, gripping Bess's hand tightly. As the words tumbled onto the page, Bess could feel Houdini's hand begin to shake. Most of the messages were simply general, loving comments such as "I miss you" or "I am fine," followed by descriptions of heaven or how happy Mrs. Weiss was. When the writing ended, the Conan Doyles were thrilled. Houdini, however, was silent.

As Houdini and Bess walked home, Bess assumed that her husband's silence and his shaking hands had been a result of the strong emotion brought on by the presence of Mrs. Weiss's spirit. Unlike Houdini, Bess firmly believed that spirits and ghosts were real. But when Bess looked into

Houdini's face as they passed beneath a street lamp, what she saw was not sentimental emotion, but clear anger.

"That was *not* my mother," Houdini said bitterly.

"But Harry, don't be such a skeptic," Bess said gently. "How can you be sure?"

"How can I be sure?" Houdini asked with a sharp laugh. "I'll tell you exactly how I can be sure. First of all, my mother was Jewish. She would never have started her message by drawing the sign of the cross. Second of all, my mother never spoke a word of English. The entire message would have been in German or Yiddish."

When Houdini and Bess reached their home, Houdini sat down on the front steps and put his head in his hands. "And last of all," he said in a small, tired voice, "if that had been my mother, she would have at least mentioned that today would have been her seventieth birthday."

After his experience with the Conan Doyles, Houdini became determined to uncover the trickery of mediums. He had experienced firsthand the pain of being fooled, and he was determined to expose these fakers who took advantage of grieving people. Although Houdini never thought that the Conan Doyles had set out to intentionally hurt him, his friendship with them would never be the same.

And so, wearing a disguise and calling himself "Mr. White," Houdini began visiting séance after séance. Night by night, the tricks he began to uncover ranged from the silly to the truly bizarre.

CHAPTER 11

"**L**ean closer, Mr. White. Sometimes the voices are but a whisper."

A famous medium in Chicago had assured Houdini, who she thought was "Mr. White," that his dead friend would speak to him—through a teakettle! Houdini felt like an idiot, leaning his ear against the spout of the kettle in order to hear a voice. But sure enough, within seconds, a faraway, whispery voice began speaking to Houdini in a vague and general way: "I miss you, my friend. All is well here on the other side . . . I will see you again one day . . ." The voice was clearly coming from inside the teakettle. Was it a spirit? Not exactly.

Upon further investigation, Houdini eventually found out how the medium did it. An assistant sat in a different room, whispering into a small transmitter. A coil in the bottom of the kettle picked up the voice vibrations, and then the voice was amplified through a telephone receiver that was carefully hidden in the spout. Basically, the medium had turned the teakettle into a tiny, one-way walkie-talkie. Today, it is hard to imagine anyone being fooled by something so simple, but in 1922, this was advanced technology.

Houdini made his notes and moved on to another séance. When the session began, the medium assured all those present that as soon as the lights were dimmed, spirits would fill the room and make their presence known through sounds. The medium went on to warn the participants that they might even feel the spirits touching them. Before the lights were turned out, the medium held hands with those sitting on either side of her. This would prove that she was not doing anything to create the sounds or the touching.

However, no one was holding the medium's feet.

In the darkness, the medium slipped a foot out of her shoe. Beneath the table, her toes grabbed a thin rope and pulled on it. Suddenly, a bell began ringing overhead. As the participants voiced their shock, the medium pulled the rope again, and several of those sitting at the table felt something lightly brush by their cheeks. Everyone was amazed and terrified—everyone except Houdini. He had read about the use of ropes at séances, and he knew what was happening. The thin rope that the medium grabbed with her toes came up through a small hole in the floor. The rope was connected to a series of small pulleys beneath the floor, and it stretched behind the walls and up to the ceiling. In the ceiling, another small hole was cut. The rope dropped through and was attached to a small bell and a box of feathers. Because the room was so dim, no one could see these two small items dangling from the ceiling. One tug rang the bell. Another stronger tug shook feathers out of the box.

Before the lights were turned back up, the medium slipped her shoe back on and kicked the rope back down into the hole in the floor. The presence of feathers around the room thrilled the séance participants even more, since birds were considered to be the carriers of spirits and souls. Clearly, a ghost or two must have flown through the room.

Another popular type of séance that Houdini investigated was known as "spirit photography." People would pay good money to have a spirit photographer take their pictures. These special "medium photographers" supposedly had the power to see ghosts and then capture them on film. People would sit in a completely empty room and have their pictures taken. But the developed pictures would show them surrounded by any number of spirits, strange lights, and objects

Because he had worked in the film industry, Houdini easily saw through these photographs. It wasn't very much trouble for the photographer to simply develop two pictures on top of each other and make two images appear at the same time. Again, this seems embarrassingly obvious to us today. But back then, trick photography was mostly unheard of—nearly everyone believed that what they saw in a picture was what had been present when the picture was taken.

"When the lights come back up, do not be afraid." The voice of a medium at yet another séance spoke sternly to those gathered around the table in the dark. "What you may see may shock you. But it is exceedingly dangerous to touch what may have appeared on the table. Touching could result in your own death."

As the lights slowly lit up the séance table, Houdini heard everyone present gasp in horror. There, in the middle of the table, was a human hand. It was a sign, the medium explained, of a spirit's presence—a part of the spirit that had re-formed itself and had been left behind.

"No! Don't touch it!" the medium shrieked as one of the participants, Mr. White, reached forward.

"I believe it is entirely harmless," he said, picking up the hand and examining it.

"Put it down—I—I . . ." the medium began.

But the medium's protests were cut short by the appearance of a police officer and a reporter. Houdini had begun bringing the law and the press with him to séances in order to expose the fake mediums and have them arrested. He pulled off his disguise and held out the hand for everyone to see.

"It is only a wax copy of a hand," he explained. "No spirits have visited this room."

In this way, Houdini began revealing the truth about phony mediums and their tricks. News of his mission to uncover the spiritualists spread across the country and even throughout Europe, where spiritualism was also popular. Before long, people were as fascinated by what Houdini would say about the spiritualists as they were about his escapes. So, never one to disappoint his fans, Houdini collected everything he had discovered about fake mediums and put it in a book called *A Magician Among the Spirits.* Then Houdini took his book and his discoveries on the road. Posters plastered up and down Main Streets across the country announced his arrival in typical Houdini fashion:

The Greatest Sensation in Years!
The Actual Exposure of a World Problem!
The Methods of Fake Mediums Brought
Before Your Eyes by . . .
HOUDINI!

After Seeing His Exhibition This Week,
You Can Have a Thousand Thrills at Home.
Be Your Own Medium!
It Is Positively Easy and Simple!

In city after city, and in small town after small town, Houdini spoke to thousands about the ways in which these so-called mediums stole money from their desperate customers. A lot of people had believed in spiritualism as if it were a religion, so they had mixed feelings about Houdini's findings. They didn't want to believe Houdini, but it was hard to ignore the facts. And, after all, Houdini's discoveries didn't mean that *all* mediums were fakes, did it? Many people were uncertain about how they felt in light of Houdini's claims.

The mediums, however, had no doubt at all about how they felt—they were furious. Some mediums truly believed they had psychic powers, while others clearly knew that what they did was a big lie. But *all* the mediums knew that they'd be out of business if Houdini kept exposing their methods. It was time for action.

"As sure as these pins go into this doll, Mr. Houdini will feel the most horrible pain!" a medium in New York shouted to a group as he performed some voodoo on a little Houdini doll.

"Dear Mr. Houdini," another psychic in the Midwest wrote, "because I have the gift of mind-reading, I know how you do all of your tricks. Please stop your cruel battle against the spiritualists, or else I will reveal all of your secrets."

Threats of lawsuits from spiritualists came in from all over the country and even from Europe. And even worse, threats of death began to show up on a weekly basis. By the end of 1924, after Houdini had been speaking about phony spiritualists for a year, the death threats reached an all-time high.

"I get letters all the time now," Houdini told a Chicago newspaper, "that predict that I am going to meet a sudden and violent death soon as a fitting punishment for what I've done."

Finally, Houdini had had enough. *All right,* he thought angrily. *If these so-called spiritualists are so determined to demand that their methods be taken seriously, then they must offer proof.* So, along with a group of doctors and scientists, Houdini formed a committee that would determine whether or not a medium could contact the dead. A highly respected magazine, *Scientific American,* offered an award of $2,500 to anyone who could prove beyond the shadow of a doubt that his or her ability to speak to ghosts was real. Immediately, a few mediums tried to fool the committee and win the money. But they were easily exposed. For a while, it seemed that there were no other mediums willing to risk their reputations. Then along came Margery.

Margery, whose real name was Mina Crandon, was the beautiful wife of a rich Boston doctor. She performed all of her séances for free, stressing that she didn't want to make money from her amazing ability to contact spirits—she just wanted to share her gift. Right away, this made her seem more sincere. Even the editors of *Scientific American* thought they might have found the real thing. Margery calmly invited Houdini and his committee to observe as many séances as they wanted. She insisted that she had nothing to hide.

What the hell is wrong with you damned scientists and magicians? Thought Houdini as he sat dumbfounded as the soft-spoken and polite Margery, who had gone into a trance at the séance, suddenly glared around the table and spoke in the deep voice of an angry man.

"You!" Margery bellowed, pointing at Houdini. "You will pay dearly for the trouble you've caused!"

Margery's husband leaned close to Houdini and whispered, "She's channeling her dead brother, Walter. This is Walter's voice you're hearing, not Margery's."

"Walter" continued to threaten and yell four-letter words at Houdini and the committee for some time. Then, suddenly, Margery went limp.

Her head fell on the table, and slowly, a white substance seemed to come pouring out of her ear until it covered her face.

"This is 'ectoplasm,'" her husband explained. "It is ghost essence—proof that her brother's ghost has possessed her body. Please don't touch it; doing so could kill Margery."

Next, the lights went out. And the same ringing of bells, tickling of falling feathers, and moving of furniture that Houdini had experienced dozens of times at séances filled the room. However, at one point, the voice of a spirit seemed to be coming through a megaphone on the other side of the room. But Houdini was holding Margery's hands. After this demonstration, Houdini had to give Margery credit. She was certainly skilled at her spiritualistic talents. But in the end, Houdini also had to expose Margery's "talents" for what they were: tricks. "Walter" was no more than a deep voice and a foul mouth perfected by the young lady. "Ectoplasm" was just wet cotton. The voice across the room had only been a well-hidden assistant. Margery was a fake. But Margery refused to admit it.

"Houdini, you son of a bitch!" screamed "Walter" as Houdini prepared to leave the final séance. "I have put a spell on you. I swear to God that you will be dead within the year!"

Houdini laughed out loud, bowed, and left the room.

More than a year later, Houdini was very much alive. He and Bess had returned to touring with his magic and escapes show. Although Houdini was now over fifty years old, he was still able to include some of his physically demanding escapes. In fact, he had even added a new escape called the Chinese Water Torture Cell. In this very famous escape, Houdini's ankles were locked in bars. Then he was turned upside down and plunged into a glass and metal cell full of water. As with the milk can trick, there were hidden latches, but it was still a difficult and dangerous stunt that required Houdini to hold his breath for nearly three minutes. Often, Houdini was exhausted after his shows.

One night in late October, 1926, Houdini sat backstage following a show for a college audience. Although Houdini was so weary that he could barely keep his eyes open, he had agreed to allow a student backstage to paint a picture of him. The student had brought along two other students who sat quietly, watching the painting come to life, while Houdini glanced through his mail.

"Mr. Houdini, I've always wondered about something," one of the students suddenly said. He was a tall, muscular young man, a boxer for the college team.

"Hmmm?" Houdini said, not looking up from his mail.

"Well, I heard that you could take a punch from anyone. Heard you were so strong that the hardest punch in the stomach can't hurt you."

Houdini wasn't really paying attention. It had been a long day, and now he was reading a letter from Bess, who had not been able to travel with him to this particular show. Houdini mumbled something and just nodded.

In a flash, the student stood up and punched Houdini as hard as he could in the stomach—*four* times. Houdini gasped and grabbed his stomach. He was in terrible pain, but he didn't want to show it. He smiled weakly at the students.

"I wasn't quite ready for that," he said, catching his breath. "But I'm fine."

The next day, Houdini was not fine. He had a burning in his stomach that felt as though he had swallowed acid. Every now and then, he would break into a cold sweat. But that didn't matter. He had to catch the train to Detroit—that night's show was sold out, and Houdini refused to disappoint an audience.

Bess met her husband at the train station. She took one look at him and was horrified. His face was practically green, sweat poured down his cheeks, and dark circles hung beneath his eyes.

"Harry! What on earth is wrong? We must go to the doctor immediately," Bess said, grabbing Houdini's arm to support him.

Houdini waved her concerns away. "No, no. Just a little tired. I'll be fine."

But before Houdini went on stage that night, Bess insisted that a doctor take a look at him. At 7:45, fifteen minutes before show time, Houdini's temperature was 104 degrees. The doctor, believing that Houdini had appendicitis, demanded that Houdini go to the hospital that very instant. Houdini refused.

"The Great Houdini does not cancel a show over a little stomachache," he scoffed.

Somehow, Houdini made it through the show. He waved and smiled and bowed to a standing ovation. But when the curtain closed, Houdini immediately fell to the floor. Hysterical, Bess ran to his side. Houdini was rushed to Grace Hospital in Detroit where it was discovered that his appendix had burst. Although his appendix was removed, it was too late. His body had been poisoned by the diseased appendix. Within the hour, the headlines of the local newspapers shouted what the doctor had quietly told Bess: "Houdini is dying."

The doctors had told Bess that it would be a miracle if Houdini could live even another twelve hours. As though willing himself to pull off one last amazing stunt, Houdini struggled through seven more days of pain. But finally, Harry Houdini looked weakly toward his wife of more than thirty years and whispered his defeat, "I'm tired of fighting." At only fifty-two, The Great Houdini was dead. Later, the spiritualists and mediums would make much of the timing of Houdini's death—it was Halloween night, 1926.

CHAPTER 12

"**Y**ou will die within the year."

"Walter" had been wrong—but only by about six months. Today, there are some who believe that Houdini's death had not been a result of appendicitis brought on accidentally by a punch. One theory is that the young man who punched Houdini was not a college student at all. Some believe that he had been part of a plot by angry spiritualists to get rid of Houdini. Others believe that Houdini had been slowly poisoned by a spiritualist who posed as an assistant. Further, they believe that doctors covered this up by blaming his death on appendicitis. Fuel was added to this murder theory when it was discovered that doctors reported removing Houdini's appendix from his left side. The appendix is on the right side of the body.

Of course, the spiritualists claimed that

Houdini brought his death upon himself by denying the presence of ghosts and spirits. The night Houdini died, a large group of spiritualists gathered at Margery's house to hear what "Walter" would have to say about Houdini's passing. But even Walter had no clear explanation. Most likely, the complete truth behind Houdini's death will remain, like many of his tricks, a mystery.

The fact is, Houdini had lived the final years of his life in quiet fear of the spiritualists. Of course, he never publicly admitted this. But even though he had devoted a lot of time and energy to exposing fake mediums, he was never completely certain that ghosts didn't exist. Maybe it was possible to return in some form after death. Maybe the spiritualists were right—maybe Houdini had angered the spirits, and now these spirits would get their ghostly revenge. Or perhaps the angry spiritualists would get their human revenge.

And so, during the last years of his life, Houdini made a plan.

"This is our code," he had said in a low voice to Bess as he handed her a slip of paper one night. "But no one, no one, must ever know this code but you."

Bess had looked at Houdini with wide eyes. "Our code . . . ?"

"Yes," Houdini had replied. "If I should die before you do, and if you should hold a séance in which these exact words are spoken by a medium, then . . ." Houdini paused, and a strange fear came into his eyes that Bess had never seen.

"Then what?" Bess had whispered.

"Then you will know it's true! You will know that it is your husband speaking to you from beyond the grave."

Bess had stared at Houdini in disbelief. "But I thought you were so certain that all these mediums were fakes. I thought you proved that spirits don't exist!"

Houdini had looked down, shaking his head. "I'm certain that the mediums I observed were phony. As far as whether or not ghosts are real—I've proven nothing."

Bess read the words on the slip of paper: *Rosabelle—answer—tell—pray answer—look—tell—answer answer—tell.* Bess understood. "Rosabelle" had been the name of the first song young Harry Houdini had heard Bess sing at her dime museum show with the Floral Sisters. Over the years, Houdini occasionally referred to Bess affectionately as "Rosabelle." Of course, only Bess and Houdini knew that. The nine other words were, in fact, part of a code that Bess and Houdini had worked out at one point in order to communicate secretly with one another, when necessary, onstage. They had assigned a certain word or pair of words for every letter of the alphabet. In this case, *answer* stood for the

letter *B*, *tell* for *E*, *pray answer* for *L*, *look* for *I*,
tell again for the letter *E*, *answer answer* for *V*,
and *tell* again for *E*.

Rosabelle believe. Tears came to Bess's eyes.
She knew that if she ever received this message
from her dead husband, she would definitely
believe.

Bess Houdini suffered greatly after her
husband's death. Since the day she had met
the twenty-year-old Harry Houdini at a dime
museum on Coney Island, her life had been
devoted to him. She had been his assistant, traveling companion, best friend, and wife for more
than thirty years. And now suddenly, much too
soon, and without any warning, he was gone.
Bess felt completely lost and abandoned.

Although Houdini had never touched a
drop of alcohol his entire life, Bess had. She had
sometimes used drinking to ease the stress of a
life in show business, though she rarely drank too
much. But now, the stress and sorrow seemed to
be more than she could bear. Bess began drinking
heavily and often combined drugs with the alcohol. Of course, the drinking and drugs only made
Bess's depression worse. Before long, she became
suicidal and attempted suicide more than once.

Somewhere in the midst of Bess's haze of
drinking and sadness, a medium named Arthur
Ford came along and took advantage of the

fragile state she was in. Or maybe he didn't. In any event, Ford somehow managed to repeat the secret code to Bess during a séance. According to reporters who were present, Bess was in bed recovering from a fall she had taken while drunk at a party. Her head was wrapped in a bandage, and she was fading in and out. However, when Ford spoke the code, she was suddenly ecstatic and shouted to the roomful of people that Houdini had been contacted. "Rosabelle, sweet Rosabelle, I love you more than I can tell. Over me you cast a spell . . ." Bess sang out from her bed before suddenly fainting from all the excitement.

Houdini Breaks Chains of Death, Talks from the Grave in Secret Code!

The news flew around the world and made the headlines of every major paper. It was a stunning breakthrough and a victory for the spiritualists. But no sooner had the news spread than new headlines appeared claiming that the whole thing had been a hoax.

"Mrs. Houdini gave me the code," Ford shrugged with a laugh. "We both thought it would be a fun publicity stunt."

"If Mr. Ford says this, I brand him as a liar!" Bess said angrily to reporters. "If anyone accuses me of giving the words that my husband gave to me, then I will fight and fight until the breath leaves my body."

The truth of the whole matter was never figured out. Somehow, Mr. Ford had gotten the code, but it had not come from the ghost of Houdini.

In the year that followed, Bess Houdini slowly pulled her life back together. She spent over a month in a sanitarium (similar to today's rehab clinics) in order to help kick her drinking problem. She specifically chose a sanitarium where "spiritualism was strictly forbidden." After her experience with Mr. Ford, she was in no mood to talk about contacting her dead husband. She had had it with mediums.

For a while, anyway.

Edward Saint was a kind and soft-spoken man who had worked in the circus for years as "The International Smileless Man." He offered $1,000 to any audience member who could make him laugh or even crack a smile. Nobody ever succeeded, regardless of how funny the jokes told might be. It wasn't that Saint had no sense of humor—his face was paralyzed! As Bess was putting her life back together, she often visited circuses and dime museums to remember the old days with Houdini. One night, she saw Saint's show and made a point to meet him. Right away, the two became good friends.

Mr. Saint lived up to his name. He helped Bess continue to fight her alcoholism. He helped her keep her affairs in order, and he made sure that Houdini's legacy was kept alive. In time, Bess became close enough to Saint to confide in him. Although her secret code with Houdini had been revealed, she still wanted to see if she could contact him.

"I have made a decision," she said to Saint one day. "I want to hold a séance again to see if Harry will speak to me in some way."

Saint nodded. He knew that Bess was still quite fragile and that too much excitement could push her over the edge again. But he could tell she had made up her mind.

"I will hold a séance every year on Halloween, the date of Harry's death," Bess continued. "If I haven't heard from him in ten years, I will stop trying."

For the next nine years, Saint faithfully put together a group of honest mediums, scientists, and close friends every Halloween night. The spirit of Harry Houdini was called upon again and again. Bess sat in the candlelight with tears in her eyes, but Houdini never answered the call.

Finally, the tenth anniversary of the Houdini séances arrived on Halloween night, 1936. The séance took place on the roof of a very tall building in Hollywood, California, where Bess was now living. It was an eerie, still night with a blood-red sunset over the Pacific Ocean. The event was to be broadcast over radio around the world. As the séance was about to begin, the guests were directed to form two circles. The radio announcer quietly described the scene: "Over three hundred invited guests formed the outer circle, while thirteen scientists, occultologists, newspapermen, world-famous magicians, spiritual leaders, and boyhood friends of Houdini joined Madame Houdini in the inner circle. Bathed in the weird glow of ruby light, everyone gathered to evoke the shade of the late mystifier." And then the séance began.

"Are you here?" the mediums shouted. "Houdini, please speak to us! This is the night of nights, and the whole world is listening. Send us some kind of sign! Ring a bell! Move a table!"

Breathless, the world waited. But the wind through the dark red sky was the only sound.

"We have waited so long, Houdini! Please, we beg of you—make your presence known!"

Still, more silence.

This went on until the stroke of midnight. Edward Saint then looked at Bess Houdini. "Mrs. Houdini, the zero hour has passed," he said quietly.

Bess sighed and looked around the circle. "Yes. Houdini did not come through. My last hope is gone. I do not believe that Houdini can come back to me—or to anyone . . . It is over and finished. Good night, Harry!"

And so Houdini would not make one last escape from the chains of death in order to send a sign to those still earthbound. Or would he?

Just as the group quietly stood to leave, a sudden bolt of lightning streaked through the night sky. A tremendous thunderclap boomed. And as Bess looked up to the heavens, a gentle autumn rain began to fall upon her face.